GOD'S NEIGHBORHOOD

A Hopeful Journey in Racial Reconciliation
and Community Renewal

SCOTT ROLEY
WITH JAMES ISAAC ELLIOTT

InterVarsity Press
Downers Grove, Illinois

The writers dedicate this book to our fathers,
Robert N. Roley
and
Harold Campbell Elliott,
who taught us the power of words.

InterVarsity Press
P.O. Box 1400, Downers Grove, IL 60515-1426
World Wide Web: www.ivpress.com
E-mail: mail@ivpress.com

©2004 by Scott Roley and James Isaac Elliott

InterVarsity Press® is the book-publishing division of InterVarsity Christian Fellowship/USA®, a student movement active on campus at hundreds of universities, colleges and schools of nursing in the United States of America, and a member movement of the International Fellowship of Evangelical Students. For information about local and regional activities, write Public Relations Dept., InterVarsity Christian Fellowship/USA, 6400 Schroeder Rd., P.O. Box 7895, Madison, WI 53707-7895, or visit the IVCF website at <www.ivcf.org>.

Interior photographs used by permission of Scott Roley.

Design: Cindy Kiple

Images: Alberto Incorcci/Getty Images

ISBN 0-8308-3224-6

Printed in the United States of America ∞

Library of Congress Cataloging-in-Publication Data

Roley, Scott
    God's neighborhood: a hopeful journey in racial reconciliation and
    community renewal/Scott Roley with James Isaac Elliott
        p. cm.
    Includes bibliographical references.
    ISBN 0-8308-3224-6 (pbk.: alk. paper)
    1. Roley, Scott. 2. Race relations—Religious
    aspects—Christianity. 3. Presbyterian Church in
    America—Clergy—Biography. I. Elliott, James Isaac, 1955-   II.
    Title.
    BX9225.R735A3 2004
    285'.176856'089—dc22
                                                                    2003027950

P	18	17	16	15	14	13	12	11	10	9	8	7	6	5	4	3	2	1
Y	17	16	15	14	13	12	11	10	09	08	07	06	05	04				

"You would need to be a minority living in a white evangelical subculture to understand fully when I say that *God's Neighborhood* is a safe place. Scott and Linda Roley are a safe place. The 'balm of Gilead' that gets down in the trenches with the wounded brother to make him whole is the balm that washes over me as I read *God's Neighborhood.*"

KIRK WHALUM, *saxophonist and recording artist*

"I recommend that every Christian read this book! It reveals the heart of a man of God who is transparent about his personal learning through his experiences in racial reconciliation and community ministries. I was blessed, encouraged and challenged to be more sensitive to all poor people."

REV. DR. BENJAMIN W. JOHNSON SR., *author, lecturer and activist*

"With the convictions of his heart and the actions of his life Scott Roley leads the church in fulfilling its biblical mission of making all believers of every people-group one in Christ. Recounting the journey that has formed his heart and led to courageous commitments is an inspiring lesson not so much about grand principles for overcoming racism as about how the simple practice of faithfully living godly priorities in a compassionate family can radically alter our world for the kingdom."

BRYAN CHAPELL, *President, Covenant Theological Seminary*

Contents

Foreword

IT'S ABOUT TWENTY-FIVE YEARS IN THE FUTURE. ON THE SHADY SIDE OF the town square of Franklin, Tennessee, sit about half a dozen older men. We sit there counting out-of-state license plates and talking about times gone by, of people and places and things that have happened to us as a company of committed brothers in the Lord.

Denny is there, complaining about his back but forever answering every query with the phrase "Blest by the Almighty." The rest of us roll our eyes—not doubting that he has been blessed, for indeed he has, but we have heard this well-worn phrase for almost forty years now. For all the decades we've known him, even in the midst of extreme suffering, this has always been his response to us. We've come to realize that even as Denny has been blessed by the Almighty, so we have been blessed by Denny. Even approaching ninety, the fire still burns in his eyes. "I'll still roll you up!" he good-naturedly threatens any of us who dare challenge him.

Mike Smith is there when he can make it. He remains the paradigm pastor of our group. He is still often off somewhere framing additions for his parishioners when his arthritis isn't bothering him, or helping a single mom get her car started, or repairing a leaking faucet, or any of a limitless number of simple tasks by which he washes all our feet with the gospel. He is in his seventies now but is nevertheless the most active of our little brotherhood.

Others come and go. Sam Judd still has a regular job and so can be here only on the weekends, though he still comes for prayer on Thursdays. Hewitt Sawyers is a regular. The story of his conversion is still one of my favorites and so he tells it over and over much to our mutual enjoyment. Basically he came to faith due to the fact that someone blocked the door before the invitation. He had always been able to sneak out before the pastor called for anyone to come down to confess and believe. Hewitt was blocked in, so what else was he supposed to do? The absurd providence of it all still makes me smile all these years later.

Off to one side sit Scott Roley and me, both bearded and somewhat bent over.

"There's my car!" I wistfully gasp as a new Jaguar rolls past.

"You've already got a car," Scott whips back, a bit irritated. We've had this discussion now nearly a thousand times. "You're Toyota still runs fine!" He's getting grumpy now.

"But still . . ." I'm lost in the image of me driving such a beautiful car.

"There goes Maine. What is he doing down here?"

Fifty years ago some of us started praying that God would give us community. A little more than forty years ago, he gave it. It was nothing like what we had anticipated. Many dreams have been shattered in the proceeding years, but God has always given us better dreams.

It started when we pledged to each other that we weren't going anywhere. We were going to resist the temptation to move away if better opportunities presented themselves to any one of us.

Later we promised that even if we disagreed with one another we would not break fellowship. Over the years we have disagreed a lot, sometimes along racial lines, more often between political positions. But the fact that we are all still here, watching cars go by, shows that our mutual promise held firm.

All during the fray, my friend Scott has been in the thick of it all. His missteps started it all. He came into Denny's predominantly black neighborhood with his youth group mowing lawns and fixing roofs as a summer project. Denny, as the pastor of the community, was understandably disappointed that Scott had not first come to him. But Scott had not understood. When Denny confronted him, Scott apologized with tears, and the two started praying together. And that was the beginning—God redeeming a situation that might have otherwise seemed unredeemable. We have prayed and wept together, married off our children and buried our close friends now for more than forty years. We're still not going anywhere. None of us is leaving.

But the sad truth is some of us have left, gone to be with the Lord, which, I realize, we should all celebrate. And a part of us did celebrate when Bill Lane or John Eaves or others "passed." But that forever human side still aches at the empty pew or the silent pause in our group prayer meetings when all of us sit and wait to hear the familiar voice of a brother whose voice we will never again hear this side of eternity.

Perhaps the best news is that there has been a steady stream of young people who've joined our ranks over the years. They are the ones who are in the thick of the battle now, who come back from the road with their own stories and requests for prayer. We, now the old guard, sit and listen and advise and pray for them, confident of the

One who was with us through so many of our battles.

Scott still lives in Hard Bargain, though the neighborhood looks nothing today like it did when he first moved into it. Slowly the little community has been renewed. House by house, family by family, a new hope has come into the neighborhood. In fact there is a growing movement to rename the community Mount Hope. That better describes it now. A new hope has slowly begun to take root in the community, a hope that Scott Roley has been talking about all these years.

"California. Can you imagine driving all that way?" Denny talks as if he had just driven all that way.

"Isn't this Thursday?"

"No, you old fool, it's Friday."

In fact, it is Thursday. And if this issue can be settled before noon, we will all proceed down to First Missionary Baptist for prayer.

We are still the men of the empty hands. We are still bound to our promise to stay put and never leave each other. But our promise has held only because we trusted in the One who always keeps his promises. If any new hopes have come to Franklin, it is not because of our fragile fellowship but in spite of it. This the older ones of us know to be true. The younger ones are in the process of learning the truth of it for themselves.

We settle that it is indeed Thursday. Our little group of old men in baggy pants trudge off, down West Main, to continue our simple task of changing the world.

Michael Card

Acknowledgments

I WANT TO FIRST THANK MY FAMILY FOR THEIR SUPPORT throughout the writing of this book. My precious wife, Linda, and our children, Matt, Emily, Michelle, Jeff and Sam, have encouraged me even when the workload left their needs unmet. Dear ones, I am undone by your unselfishness. I hope I can communicate how deeply I love you.

Michael Card's involvement gave me the opportunity to publish this book. He has suggested more helpful ideas than I could write down. Our close relationship over twenty years has been my joy and privilege. Thank you, Michael, for defining me. I am honored by your friendship.

My discipler since 1978 has been Scotty Smith. He has pastored my family and our community. I am grateful to Christ Community Church for teaching me the gospel and challenging me to live missionally. Scotty, we have been together for more than a thousand Sundays and I don't see any reason to change.

From my past I'm thankful to Ray Husband for his skillful and caring conversations leading me to believe in Christ.

Bill Lane and Jack Miller taught me to love the Bible, resulting in the desire for a lifestyle of repentance, mercy and worship.

In the late 1960s, friendships with Steve Vanker, Howard Tryon, Ron Kopicko and Ted Kallman challenged me to pursue creativity, discovering that exploring all areas of life was a good thing.

To my mother Joan Henson and my sisters Laurie Louis and Beth Landau, I am overwhelmed by how fortunate I am to be your son and brother. I only regret we could not spend more time together over the years. I am so proud of you.

I am indebted to Denny Denson, Hewitt Sawyers, Walter Amos, Lynn Owens and other members of the Empty Hands Fellowship for teaching me about African American heritage and culture. You have given your hearts to me as true brothers. I would not be who I am if we had not been called to build loving relationships of repentance and forgiveness.

The establishment of Franklin Community Ministries through the tireless effort of Paige Overton Pitts and its continuation through Cady Wilson and Terri Norris established the vehicle for community development in my life. I am humbled by your willingness to give away credit and praise in order to build God's neighborhood.

Pastor Chris Williamson and Strong Tower Bible Church have demonstrated what racial reconciliation in Southern culture is all about. I cannot overemphasize the importance of this church to the creation of a new Franklin and a new South. Thank you for your patience and for continually challenging me to wait on the Lord, remembering the results are up to God.

Author Bill Crew helped me find my voice as a writer, and his instruction gave me confidence to keep writing.

Sara Elliott was a wonderful addition to our team, contributing early editorial advice leading to the completion of this book.

My stepparents Millie and Bill McIntosh have always stood by my Christian faith and witness. They have parented me by supporting my family's faith-based lifestyle.

My brother Jeff Roley has been with me throughout my life, and we share not only the heritage of family but also brotherhood in Christ. Jeff, I cannot imagine still being alive without your prayers for me. By God's grace we will continue our days believing in a gospel-driven lifestyle through words and deeds. Thank you for being my true brother.

To my friend James Elliott, I am grateful we sat down that day at the Waffle House in Nashville and reviewed a few pages of what is now this book. You really did believe we could finish the project, and I am thankful for your endurance and reassuring voice.

Finally, to Jeff Crosby and Al Hsu along with all my new friends at IVP. Thank you for taking a chance on me and this book. God bless you in all your work.

Scott Roley
Franklin, Tennessee
January 2004

Introduction

The Least of These

IT WAS A COLD WINTER EVENING, BUT IT WAS WARM INSIDE THE Nashville Rescue Mission where Michael Card and I were serving food, preaching, singing and doing dishes for several hundred weary souls who, after listening to us, were guaranteed a bed for the night. The audience really didn't tune in to the program. They seemed more satisfied to sit in a pew or bench seat just because it eased the burden of carrying their weight and gave them shelter from the frigid weather.

An elderly, heavy-set woman entered the small chapel amidst coughing and sneezing and muffled muttering. She looked haggard and worn out. It was difficult to tell if she was truly overweight or just loaded down under the three or four tattered overcoats she was wearing. I was in front of the group, who were talking loudly and being unruly.

She came forward slowly. I was singing a newly composed song about unborn children. Her bulky form shuffled in front of me, casting her shadow across my guitar in such a way as to demand immediate attention. She stood over my lyric sheet weeping, her tears hitting the song chart on the music stand and running down the manuscript, blurring the words.

My first thought was that maybe if she just backed up I could finish this song and get on with caring for people. Then I looked her in the eyes. She was African American, old, poor, alone, weary and deeply sad. Embarrassed, I put my guitar down and moved the music stand to face her. As I asked her to tell me her troubles, it was as if the message of God meeting us in *the least of these* became incarnate, became real.

She said, "I need to tell you something." As she spit out her story, the sadness in her voice drew me in. "One of my daughters had an abortion, and I lost my only grandchild," she said, the pain still fresh in her heart. She continued her story, telling me that during the procedure her daughter's uterus was perforated. So not only would there be no baby, but the hope for future children and grandchildren was gone forever. The broken woman labored to finish, repeating phrases and forgetting where she was.

I thought of several spiritually clever answers to comfort her, maybe "Jesus loves you," or "All things work together for good." Any Scripture might have been appropriate. What could I say? Something in me told me not to speak, but instead to reach out. I put both of my awkward arms around her and pulled her close to me in a bear hug that made us look like two Eskimos slow dancing. I put my face right next to hers, cheek to cheek. I felt her warm tears still flowing and actually started to cry myself. I'd never been that close to a black woman. We held each other lamenting her loss and crying for a while as the people in the room, completely unaware of us, went on about their business.

Michael watched the whole thing. He spoke tenderly to me afterward, saying, "You know she saw Christ in you?" It hadn't occurred to me, but that seemed to be true. He went on, "Yes, she did, and that is a profound miracle to be Jesus' representative with arms and tears and love. But the greater miracle, if that's possible, is not that she saw Christ in you. It is that you met Christ in her."

An elderly poor black woman and a young white aspiring activist artist combined to form a reality that was simple and complex. When Jesus said to love the least of these, he meant to love in both word and deed. Jesus relocated, and calls us to follow. His creative connectional reneighboring would demand action. Connectional reneighboring was Jesus' method of coming to earth incarnate—his creation became his neighborhood.

God's Neighborhood is a book about my journey in racial reconciliation and community renewal through a variety of societies living out a daily vision to love God and his people. I am a white pastor at a large Presbyterian church in Franklin, Tennessee.

Several years ago my wife, Linda, and I moved our family, which included an adopted African American son and a mixed-race son, into an African American neighborhood called Hard Bargain. We were responding to a call God placed in my heart to find new neighbors and "love them as I love myself." I have partnered with some African American pastors and other brothers and sisters whose hearts have been warmed by the gospel to seek ways to serve our community as we serve one another.

For many years Michael Card and others have encouraged me to tell my story, and I turned to my longtime friend and brother, James Isaac Elliott, for help. I met James when he was a college student in Michigan, and we immediately connected. He followed me to Nashville where we wrote songs and played music together. Today he is a professor and an award-winning songwriter whose compositions have been recorded by dozens of artists, including Steven Curtis Chapman. He was a founding member of Christ Community Church and has been a part of my life the past three decades.

I am telling this story from a small-town, southern American context, and to the reader it might not fit every experience in race-related situations. However, each one of us has a life lesson to learn about relating to people who are different. Wherever the salient point of conflict exists, God's people are called to love. For instance, there is profound racial tension among ethnic and religious factions within the Pacific Northwest, New England and Southern California. That strife is obviously not just between black and white people. Hatred among those groups seems unrelated to our struggles in Franklin, but confronting that conflict is the priority for people living in those regions.

It was Scotty Smith's vision to start a church in Franklin, and I was excited when he invited me to join him in the new adventure. From humble beginnings Christ Community Church has grown to several thousand members. We have many high-profile people living in our city, and on any given Sunday you might see singers like Michael Card, Steven Curtis Chapman, Steve Green, Geoff Moore, Alison Krauss, Buddy Green, Vince Gill, Amy Grant or members of the band Jars of Clay. Others who worship with us include bestselling author Peter Jenkins and racing great Daryl Waltrip. We are all seeking to find our place in the community of faith as we love and support one another.

The word *community* gets tossed around like it is something immediately understood. For instance, we love our community, we need our community, and we must protect our community. Yet the word is somewhat vague and undefined. As Christians we recognize the Bible teaches that we are to live our lives together as God's people. I discovered salvation is not simply an individual experience. It is rather additionally a corporate experience. God has said in Scripture, "I will be their God and they will be my people."

The work of Christian community required me to heed God's call in Scripture to care for the poor. It became difficult to ignore Jesus' mandate to love the poor. He clearly demonstrated this love by saving us from the destruction of our sin and restoring us to himself. I believe any Christian community worth talking about will come to understand and care about poverty, both in spirit and in material goods.

My personal journey into community renewal started as a young man witnessing the social turmoil of the early 1960s. I saw my need for truth and began to respond to it. Social justice, race relations, and care for the poor stirred my conscience. As I grew over the years, my ideas changed about every one of these issues. God led me through each transition. The journey was, is and always will be demanding of faith.

Christ's cross is a reminder of God's mercy. It is not always clear how the death of the Son of God remains the high point of our journey—his poverty substituted for ours, his life given for ours. But the hope for true community, though sometimes hard to grasp, is real and found in him alone. *God's Neighborhood* is about understanding and participating in Christian community. It describes a response to the biblical mandate of care for the poor.

This response manifests itself specifically through racial reconciliation, creative connectional forms of reneighboring, and the empowerment of disinherited people. These categories are adaptations of John Perkins's classic community development strategies of reconciliation, relocation and redistribution.

As I read John Perkins's books *Let Justice Roll Down* and *With Justice for All*,[1] God opened my eyes to the needs beyond the difficult circumstances of *at risk* communities staring us in the face. We must look into the eyes of poverty and examine the heart, soul and psyche of it. People aren't just in need of drug rehab, a roof over their heads or decent food to eat. They also require the dignity of true and relevant education, affordable health care, and living wage opportunities. John Perkins's holistic approach to community development was unlike anything I'd ever heard.

I first learned about Dr. Perkins through a video his ministry produced in Mississippi to promote Christian community development. Michael Card and I were traveling the country performing music concerts, and the tape had been given to us to view on the tour bus when we got bored. We watched it once, and it changed our lives. It immediately reinforced messages of caring for the poor that I heard as a child from leaders like John and Robert Kennedy. It also supported the concept of racial reconciliation, which was taking hold of me after listening to civil rights architects like Dr. Martin Luther King Jr.

I first heard the term *reneighboring* from the community developer Bob Lupton, referring to the work he was doing in an underserved community of Atlanta, Georgia.[2] This kind of creative language helped all of us to get the big picture of Christian community development.

My prayer is that you will be inspired, encouraged and challenged as you read this book. I hope that your heart will be moved to find your place in God's neighborhood as you discover how he has worked in my life. May God bless you on your journey.

1   King and Kennedy

I PUSHED OPEN THE FRONT SCREEN DOOR AND JUMPED UP ON the waist-high brick wall that wrapped around the front porch of my boyhood home on Rucker Place in an elite neighborhood of Alexandria, Virginia. Balancing myself and walking along the top of it until I got to the sunny corner, I hung on to the square pillar and, like always, leaned out as far as possible while looking north toward the city. From that corner of the porch, a providential crevice between the canopies of the trees gave me a good look at the glimmering white dome of the Capitol building several miles away in Washington, D.C. The dome would always redirect my thoughts, and even without books and teachers I knew it was important and special. The corner spot was my own secret observation post, and it was what made my house the best on the block.

That August day I realized I was one month away from starting the sixth grade. So I went back inside and lay down on the wide living room floor to drift into my favorite daydream by tossing my football up toward the ceiling and catching it. I pretended to be a star quarterback when it went up and a great receiver when it came down.

From there I heard the phone ring, and the tone of my mother's voice that followed made it obvious that something was happening.

She got my older brother Jeff from our bedroom and me from the floor, and before we could fuss properly about being disturbed, our shirts were changed, our faces were wiped, and our hair was slicked back with butchwax. While rushing us through her two-handed spit shine she gave us instructions, some change, and a kiss and hurried us out of the house to the public bus stop two blocks away on King Street. We barely caught the bus and our breath, crowding together on the hot seat and pulling down the window for some fresh air. The door slapped shut, the air brakes sighed, and the bus pulled away headed for the city.

I HAVE A DREAM

In thirty minutes we were there. Jeff and I had taken the public bus from Alexandria to Washington many times before, but today it was packed with more people than usual, and it took a little longer to get there. When the bus finally stopped we could see the center of Washington, and even though we had been to many downtown events like Redskins games at the stadium, we had never seen a crowd of people like the one forming ahead. A mass of young and old black people streamed down the wide street toward the middle of the capital. Everyone was exiting the bus slowly. I remember the people bending over and staring out the windows at the crowd as they moved to the front, looking hesitant about leaving whatever safety the bus provided.

Jeff and I, following the other riders, got off and started making our way through the somber, determined people who were quietly singing, humming and obviously waiting for something. We didn't know what was going on downtown, but we were both Boy Scouts, and good Scouts learn to compile their clues and make reasonable assumptions, especially while they're walking.

Carving our way west, we easily solved the small mystery in which we found ourselves: Mom rushing us out the door after the phone call, Dad wanting us at his office immediately, a full bus, too many police, and the large crowd. It could all mean only one thing. Dad's impromptu enthusiasm for learning, history and events in this city provided our lives with a certain cultural electricity, and we concluded that he had learned of some once-in-a-lifetime occurrence that he would be sure to explain to us in detail. His many stories about Washington included the recounting of marches and rallies, and the signs some members of the crowd carried confirmed our deductions. Something special was going to happen in the nation's capital today. The only thing we didn't know was what this gathering was all about and why there were so many black people. Jeff was my leader, and he told me, "We've got to move fast. This crowd will sweep us away if we don't watch out."

Our hurried hike continued. Many times we had traveled the history-lined blocks from the bus terminal in front of the Treasury Department to the building where our father worked on Pennsylvania Avenue. Visiting him in the city was one of our favorite things to do. The attention to civic detail that prompted his excited phone calls also made him ensure that we knew the name and function of all the federal buildings that we passed along the way. He taught us how to find our way to his office from almost anywhere in Washington, and having inherited his adventurous tendencies, we liked knowing that we could do it and that Dad trusted us to get there.

This time, as we walked the familiar territory, I was aware of an unmistakable contrast between the throngs in the streets and the sights that marked our way. Countless black people were traversing the center of the capital, but we saw no black monuments or statues anywhere. People came from all over the world to see Washington's historical buildings, but nothing the tourists came for represented these black men walking around wearing pressed white shirts, skinny black ties and woven porkpie hats.

Simplemindedness led me to wonder whether all these visitors were now disappointed or if that was why all the black people were here; they had no statues of their own. That seemed unfortunate in a Washington that was big enough to include them if it wanted to. Maybe that's what Dad meant when he said that things were changing around here. Jeff and I argued about which turn to make as the statues and monuments seemed to come alive pointing the way.

I didn't care if black people had a thousand of their own monuments as long as they didn't make them so big that the view from my front porch was ruined. Dad told us that buildings in the city weren't allowed to be as tall as those in New York and Chicago because nothing could be high enough to hide the Capitol. He enjoyed reiterating that the second greatest reason to come and see him was that when we went to his twelfth floor office in the Pennsylvania Building we got the longest possible elevator ride in all of Washington.

That was okay, but the Howard Johnson's restaurant on the ground floor of his building was the real drawing card. For years it had been all the incentive we needed to pay Dad a visit, and it was far more exciting than all the monuments, pillars and elevators. After looking in the door of our favorite lunch counter and counting the available stools, we would fight over the right to push the buttons that started the long elevator ride to the top floor of the building and walk down the hall to Dad's office.

Sometimes he wasn't done with his work when we got there, so he would give us some quarters and let us go back down to the Howard

Johnson's for hot dogs, cheeseburgers and orange freezes. Spending our change there was a lot more fun than handing it over to a bus driver, and we always hoped that when we arrived Dad still had plenty of work to do. When we got off the elevator that day, people in the hallway pressed up against the windows looking out at the streets below. Dad was waiting for us in his office with a big smile. The commotion in the halls didn't bother us at all because we saw him reach in his pocket, and that meant it was time for cheeseburgers.

Just as we were finishing our freezes, Dad came and gathered us off our spinning stools and led us outside to walk through the crowd again, this time all together. Using his unique command of words and inflection that always forced us to think and then think again, he explained the large gathering while we walked toward the Lincoln Memorial from 13th Street. He slowly and purposefully weaved us through the crowd until we reached a spot by one of the tall washed marble platforms intermittently placed around the Reflecting Pool.

The pedestal was shoulder high, and Dad boosted Jeff and me up to sit on the empty space on top. Our legs dangled over the sides. He gestured toward the men standing on a stage built in front of the sitting statue of Abraham Lincoln and pointed out one particular man, sharp eyed and eager, seemingly more important than the rest of them standing there. "His name is King," he said. I can still see the snapshot my mind took of that moment: my father pointing in the foreground, Martin Luther King Jr. and history in the background.

Our means of measuring just about everything in life was a football field, and the platform where the speakers gathered was one perfect gridiron away from our sun-scorched pedestal. At that time King was a stranger to us, but we were about to find out who he was. More and more people were squeezing into the packed area, shuffling with expectation, and keenly interested in someone or something that was about to happen. Their sweat-glazed faces were intent on somehow finding a future in the midst of a crowd that was big enough to deny one's identity instead of providing it.

It was hot. Dad was still in his suit and was regularly wiping the sweat from his forehead and trying to estimate the size of the crowd. Not even an astute political observer like my father could have foreseen how many millions of searching feet would be trampling across the same soil over the next decade as this plot of ground shook under millions of marchers, liberty seekers and college dropouts. I sometimes long to be granted the ability to see that August gathering through adult eyes. In years to come I wondered if any of the hopeful black participants around me that day were the same ones I saw on television getting scattered by German shepherds in Birmingham and knocked off their feet by water gushing from fire hoses in Montgomery, Alabama.

Dad helped us put on the two-color metal buttons that were distributed to the marchers: a drawing of a black hand shaking a white hand with some words about jobs and union information written underneath. King was introduced, and everybody cheered with fervor that I had only heard out of loyal Redskins fans on Sunday afternoons. He came out to the front of the group and stood behind the microphone, and even though we were still anticipating more information to help us understand, most in the crowd seemed to know who he was already.

After he waved he started to speak. He was wearing a suit like Dad and one of the same black-and-white buttons we had on. He looked right at the people and talked like someone born to speak, a solitary voice inspiring silence from others. Even my young ears knew there was something different and powerful about the words King was saying. "When we let freedom ring from every village and every hamlet, from every state and every city, we will be able to speed up that day when all of God's children, black men and white men, Jews and Gentiles, Protestants and Catholics, will be able to join hands and sing in the words of the Old Negro spiritual, 'Free at last! Free at last! Thank God Almighty, we are free at last!'"[1]

I know the words well now. The speech has been branded on American history and conscience through the combustible blend of the truth in the words and the climate that they were thrown into. What I heard spoken then was not all within my range of interest and understanding, but it was riveting enough to chase away the fidgety habits of young hands and feet.

King talked about the shadow of Abraham Lincoln and Negroes that were still not free. He talked about Mississippi and New York, and he talked about voting. He talked about white children and black children living together as neighbors and he talked about justice and freedom. The voices around me responded with "that's right" and "ummhumm" and "amen" while he was talking. King sounded like a zealous football coach to me at the time, but the people acted like they were in church. Dad wasn't wiping his sweat anymore. He was just listening, and like everybody else seemed happy right where he was. Even though we almost broke our necks to get there, King was not in a hurry, and no one was rushing to get anywhere now.

It seemed as if a few minutes after he started, it was over, and King was waving goodbye. My father got us down from our perch, and we started to walk through the people again, not talking as much during the walk back to his office as when we came. He did ask some questions about what we heard, and he talked about things that were not as they should be. Some of his gentle explanations and words passed over me as King's did, but the sobriety that seemed to grip adults whenever they discussed equality hinted at the depth of it all. I knew it was okay that I did not understand because Dad made it sound as if no one else really did either.

What I did hear clearly was a simple truth that seemed to be the whole point of the conversation with my father and King's speech: America was founded on certain truths and rights, but now it was time to wrestle with them. Weighty words that had been applied to paper and not society would someday have to be either lived out or erased. Ideas that were supposed to be self-evident remained veiled and undiscovered.

Dad said that we would probably see King again, and he told us we should watch television that night and save the buttons on our chest. I did. It remains one of my prized possessions today.

JFK

Just a few days after I saw King, I entered the sixth grade at Matthew Fontaine Maury Elementary School, three blocks away from our house near the corner of Masonic View and King Street in Alexandria. The only positions that were important to me were on the football and basketball teams and in the next level of Boy Scouts; but in the third week of school, class leaders were picked, and I was chosen as the new chairman of the school social work committee.

There were no write-in ballots for young renegades like me, so my father's job as a Commerce Department patent attorney and my habit of asking what the teachers called unanswerable questions probably got me selected. I didn't have much of an opinion about the committee, and I didn't know if I would like being a part of it or not. We met at school and learned the meaning of words like *sociology, society,* and *poverty,* and we made plans to do things outside the shelter of our school building. After our initial attempt at a local canned food drive, school faculty told me that President John F. Kennedy would be hosting a special luncheon at the White House to personally honor all the school-based social-work committees in the Washington area. They told me that as chairman I would be representing the committee and our school at the lunch in the second week of November. I knew I would like that.

The weeks went quickly, and the day arrived when I was on my way to have lunch with the President. The Capitol dome sparkled in the morning sun, and my heart beat a little faster as the White House came into view. As it turned out it was even more than my parents said it would be. Even a young middle-school student could discern the pervasive sense of history on those grounds. It was startling to realize that when I looked at all of the windows, trees, steps and lights—at anything—I was looking at things that great presidents and world leaders had also laid eyes on.

Kennedy was walking around on the most pristine, beautiful lawn that I had ever seen with a small entourage of important-looking people. He waved to the students, and a White House employee who was our event chaperone said the President would be speaking with us after our lunch. Long tables were prepared and decorated just for us, a gathering of elementary school students who had been told we had a future in social work. Our young activism and small accomplishments were only recent occurrences, and none of us knew each other. Yet for some reason being at the White House that day made us all act as if we did.

It was probably one of the best lunches I've ever eaten, but I have no idea what we were served, and I wasn't the only kid not paying attention to it. We were there to see and hear John F. Kennedy, the leader of the free world. Soon after our dessert was cleared, the tense, formal chaperone told us to stand up. A less fretful President came right over to our tables and immediately asked us to sit back down. Understandably, he was instantly heroic to me, and he never really had to earn it. In later years, I attempted to separate the flattering image of Kennedy inspired by my youthful awe from the pragmatic and reasonably critical view of people and politics that comes from the perspective of time and reading newspapers.

Kennedy said that he was proud of us and thankful that Washington and America had kids like us to count on. He told us that what we were doing in our schools and our communities made America the best country in the whole world. He had goals that he wanted to accomplish, he said, and he could not achieve them without citizens like us. Kennedy smiled a lot, and he made the White House seem less like a monument and more like a house. I wondered if the President and Dr. King were friends, since both of them were important and liked being outside in Washington talking to people.

When it was time for Kennedy to shake our hands everyone got excited, and the nice straight rank that the chaperone put us in got a little sloppy. The President had to adjust to our eagerness. He cheerfully tried to shake every small hand thrust in his direction, crossing his arms left over right and right over left as he walked down the line shaking and smiling. Every now and then a kid would get skipped by his method, and I was one of them. I might have been disappointed, but he only missed my hand because he looked me in the eyes. His suit jacket brushed up against mine too, so it didn't matter that my hand wasn't shaken.

After he passed by I looked down and saw that Kennedy's oxford had made a clean fresh imprint in the plush grass right in front of me. I didn't want to walk away from that spot because I knew that his footprint must be significant. All I could do was stare at it. While looking down I remembered all the footprints in the grass around the Reflecting Pool in August and was reminded of a story my dad told me more than once.

When my dad was seven years old my grandfather took him on a visit to Calumet Farms, the renowned horse-breeding ranch in Kentucky. While they were exploring the barns, a muscular horse was walked by, and my granddad asked the man holding the reins if that was the famous Man O' War. The man said yes, and my grandfather explained to my dad how important Man O' War was. His words must have been inspiring, because my dad reacted to the information by reaching down and grabbing a handful of grass from the middle of Man O' War's hoof print. He placed that grass in a small vial, and it has remained in our family as a keepsake ever since.

That recollection gave me more to do than just wonder. I quickly reached down, grabbed a tuft of grass from the Kennedy footprint, and put it in my jacket pocket. President Kennedy's tracks may not have been as deep as Man O' War's, but there was no doubt that they were better. I couldn't wait to show my Dad, and I resolved to refuse the trade if he offered to swap his keepsake for mine.

Our White House luncheon included the music and marching of the Black Watch Band from Scotland, invited to play for the President before he was to leave Washington on a trip to Dallas, Texas.[2] After Kennedy addressed us about serving our country through the work we were doing and encouraged us that we too might become presidents, he disappeared to a second-floor balcony to sit with his family.

The band came out soon after in their striking red and black uniforms and got in ranks that were much straighter than our handshaking line. When they raised their instruments, their music pierced the cheerful mood on the lawn. I recognized the haunting sounds from home, where the bagpipes and flutes of my father's recordings were accompanied by subdued lighting and the smell of pipe tobacco almost always leading to a proud storytelling session about his Scottish heritage. The music belonged in that setting at home, but at the

White House it sounded like it was straining to serve the sunny day and the smiling President. Looking back, the stark contrast between the ominous music and the bright setting was almost prophetic. Since talking was temporarily suspended, I just reached in my pocket and felt the grass, knowing that, bagpipes or not, I would never forget this day.

School was a lot more important to me after that. With fresh enthusiasm I looked forward to doing the things that Kennedy said meant so much to him and to America. By November I was not only the head of the social-work committee at Maury Elementary but also a patrol boy complete with badge and patrol belt. When the small rotation brought my turn, I would guide pedestrian students and help direct traffic around the school during the day.

Most of the time not much happened while I was waving kids and cars around, but one week after my lunch at the White House two police cars with flashing lights appeared right near the spot where I usually stood for patrol. I remember their car doors being swung wide open and a loud, static-distorted voice coming from the radios inside. The police officers looked odd. Their hats were off, and they were slouching against their cars, rubbing their heads, and listening intently to whatever was coming over the radio.

I approached them, and they looked over at me as I walked toward my regular spot. I'm not sure why I had the will to approach them and ask what was wrong. They straightened their backs but not their faces, and they told me that the President had been shot in Dallas, Texas. One of them said that things didn't look real good for him. They told me to concentrate on my duty and that my mother and father would tell me more about it that evening. I walked away from them and stood in my spot, ready to be alert and give good signals as if I had not heard the disturbing news. But I didn't understand how a shooting like that could happen. I spent the rest of my time out on the street noticing how few cars were driving around, peering at the mortified officers, and pondering another mystery: *Why weren't all of those police and safety officers who were always surrounding the President able to prevent this tragedy?*

After I finished my patrol I went into the school building and found the halls full of crying teachers and dazed students. We did no class work the rest of the day. I wanted to get out of there and go home so I could talk to my mom and dad about what had happened. My parents did talk to me more about it that night, but it only made things worse. I had never seen them both so sad and unable to say something funny to make me and them feel better. They said there was nothing to say that could change the fact that President Kennedy was coming back to Washington in a casket.

A heavy sadness now mingled with my memories of him looking at me and brushing up against me and of saving grass from the White House lawn. My parents wore the same expression I had seen all afternoon in school. They were getting from the television the same thing that we got from the teachers at school, lots of words but no real explanations or answers. I was tired and confused, so I went to bed.

Years later, while I was reading the speech President Kennedy was to deliver in Dallas, God's sovereignty and providence stood out.

> We in this country, in this generation, are by destiny rather than choice the watchman on the walls of world freedom. . . . And that we may achieve in our time and for all time the ancient vision of peace on earth, good will toward men. That must always be our goal. . . . For as it was written long ago, *except the Lord keep the city, the watchmen waketh but in vain.*[3]

Those three months between August and November left me with

feelings that could not fit on a football field, and I had no idea where the next first down marker was. Kids my age and breed didn't have transparent discussions with each other, so I didn't know how many kids felt the way I did. I bet a lot of them did. Life had been nothing but sports, scouting, and fun, but during that time even a sixth grader could see that for many people life offered hardship and burden.

Children who feel safe only because the adults look secure need only wait awhile to see those expressions change. There was another world wrapped all around the one I lived in, and the fracture that had occurred between them was letting the sadness and the reality of that world creep in and the carefree spirit of mine slip out.

Just as the Capitol dome found its way to my front porch through a gap between the trees, a new darker realm had squirmed uninvited into my life. The sources of joy that I had known were still there, but they were forced now to share space with my new awareness of the troubles that were a defining part of life. There were black people who knew too much scorn and too little freedom, children who needed other children to deliver canned green beans for them to have dinner, haunting bagpipe music, and men who kill presidents in the world.

My young view of that world from a hill in Alexandria was changing. My father was right when he said that things would be different and that the world changes in one way and people in another. Not even my elementary school, a bastion of optimism and excitement, was spared from the effects of America's tensions and troubles. From the morning arrival until afternoon dismissal an injured, questioning mentality walked the halls with the teachers and students, cooling any efforts at happiness with reminders that calamity can show up anywhere at any time.

The reciting of the pledge of allegiance was still one of my favorite parts of the day, but it now sounded more like wishful thinking than a patriotic dedication. We used to ignore the serious yellow and black signs on the walls that told us where to go if Russia fired her missiles at Washington, but now we memorized every word and regularly practiced hiding in the school basement. I wondered if the Redskins would ever be able to play well again, and if next year's football cards would show the players' faces wearing the same strained look everyone else wore—a gaze that said tomorrow was not to be trusted. The white Capitol dome could still be seen from my porch, but it had lost some of its luster. I had discovered that for many people, *America* was a painful word.

It was the first time that I remember wanting to talk to God, the Almighty who was revered in our scouting pledges and who was bigger than the sky. He was wise and good and willing to show those attributes to small people like me. He could tell me if I wasn't ready for the sixth grade or if I would just have to be. Although my age offered me much joy I recognized that my heart was grabbing for responses to my own unanswerable questions. *What providence placed me in a neighborhood close enough to Washington to view the Capitol dome? What should I be learning, seeing, thinking?*

King and Kennedy seemed larger than life at first, but when I saw them next to the harsh realities of my world, they were also vulnerable. To me they went from being virtually unknown to being big and then back to small again, the same mental reduction that happened to Superman when I found out about kryptonite. *What kind of hero has to depend on reasoning with people about freedom or gets shot down in the street? What kind of hero changes people with words and then dies unjustly in broad daylight? Does God want heroes to suffer that kind of transformation in the minds of others, and is he the only one unshaken*

by what was happening in Washington? If so, *he* could help me understand why I was pulled out of my own afternoon daydreams to go
and listen to a black man tell me about his—and why some part of
me was stirred by my encounter with a President who was laid to
rest three weeks later.

2   Virginia

MY FAMILY HAD A MEMBERSHIP AT THE SEGREGATED WOODLAWN
Country Club, where I spent my summers swimming, playing golf
and signing snack bar bills as if I were the son of a monarch. The only
black people we saw were on their way to someone's house to work
or on their way back home, to the other side of the tracks.

My first memories of black people are a kaleidoscope of images
that blend together and come into focus in one vision:

*A mysterious solitary man makes his way along the edge of town. He
walks across my imagination at an aimless pace, either his own or one I
somehow invent for him. He is not in any hurry as he follows the old railroad tracks eastward into the burning midday sun. Or he could be walking
beside a quiet lazy river, or simply the debris of modern life. The faded colors of his humble clothes suit him. His coat is grossly oversized, and he
shuffles in baggy pants as if to unheard music. As he makes his way, he
looks down at his rolled-up pant legs and the impressions his bare feet
make in the dirt more often than he looks up to the sky, as if he, like me, is
trying to see where he is going. His footprints are bigger than any I've ever
seen—even Jack Kennedy's oxford impressions on the White House lawn*

couldn't compare. I watch him in the distance, hoping to get closer, wonder-
ing what his life is like. I ponder the unknowns of where he came from,
where he would sleep that night, what he would eat for supper, what kind
of toothpaste he used. What was his neighborhood like? Did he have a nice
lawn where he played football? Did he know Dr. King? Did Martin Luther
King Jr. know him?

The bright image prompted hope for the man and his journey. Maybe its only purpose was to remind me and others that he was supposed to be here.

Those images of the first black people I saw burned into my mind: Men who were as dark as the darkest cave, eyes like black marbles set in a dish of cream. I didn't know how to look at them. I wondered what they thought when looking at me. All my usual paths were blocked. The darker the men or women, the stronger the inclination I had to ignore them. Somehow I was afraid, but I didn't know why. *Why did so many people think they were bad, just because their skin was a different color?*

Why was I drawn to the black man in my vision? Something intrigued me about his life. The way others are drawn by space, the depths of the ocean or drugs, I was drawn to these ones with skin darker than mine. It was a peculiar attraction, absurd and threatening. It was growing alongside so many other interests that were easier to under-stand, things that were generally beneficial to me and me alone. But no matter how much satisfaction I was having in my own universe, a part of me yearned to reach into his. This traveler or neighbor seemed to be outside my world, and some unknown growing flicker within me was trying to change that. I had a sense of wanting to con-nect, wanting to communicate.

But how do you communicate if you don't know the language? The barrier of race, the darkness, the blackness, the unspoken untouchability continued to rob me. Where was this black man going? It was clearly not right to ignore him. I was missing out on the wisdom of his experiences. I wanted to touch his skin, hear his thoughts, learn to listen to his accent, walk like him, talk like him, live like him. He was unapproachable and inviting at the same time. I knew little or nothing of the brokenness being lived out in front of me through lives that had no privilege, not even the right to vote. My carefree days as a country club kid arrogantly ordering cold drinks from black servants were coming to a close. I was being led in a new direction.

RFK

Those earliest images began my journey. They compelled me to want to do something about injustice. Reverend King moved me. I wanted to help. I heard the cries of his countrymen, my countrymen. I saw from afar the miserable poverty. I knew it wasn't right. I also saw the random smiles. I heard the joy in the songs he sang and in the carefree prayers offered up with confidence that the Creator is listening. I wanted to sing. I wanted to pray. I wanted to be like him. There was hope in the sadness.

It was a hope that seemed firm and secure but fragile at the same time and that almost shattered for good when Dr. Martin Luther King Jr. was assassinated on a downtown Memphis motel balcony by a demented racist named James Earl Ray. The year was 1968, and King was in Tennessee doing what he liked to do best, helping the poor. The Memphis area garbage collectors strike was his incentive to go and serve his people.

Only God knew it would be his last assignment. It was the coldest, darkest news that any part of us holding out for *good* news could hear. Hearts broke everywhere. There was a vast global wave of sadness felt with despair any place people were trying to make a difference. How could it be? How could he be dead? And so it was as if by decree through some dreadful coronation that the spring and summer of 1968 brought into view the other Kennedy, the younger brother, as he was crowned the new reconciler and caretaker of the poor, a young prince devoted to empowering the disinherited.

Robert Kennedy believed in civil rights. He had been the nation's feisty attorney general when I visited the White House back in the fall of 1963. It hadn't been the same after his brother died.

I was fourteen years old in the fall of 1966 when I met Robert Kennedy. The father of one of my friends at school was a lawyer who helped Robert and Ethel Kennedy with a small legal matter. Well, maybe it wasn't that small, but it seemed to make a good story.

The Kennedys loved horses, and Ethel Kennedy didn't like the way a neighbor was caring for his horses. She thought they were being underfed and mistreated, so she took the situation into her own hands. Actually, she took the horses into her own hands. Mrs. Kennedy "rescued" the starving ponies from the mean neighbor. She literally went over to the adjacent fields and got the horses, brought them back to her barn, fed them, and kept them overnight in her stalls.

As you might imagine, the neighbor was not too happy about that. He sued the Kennedys for taking the horses. I remember seeing a western one time where some guys did something like that and they called them "horse thieves." Somehow calling Mrs. Kennedy a "horse thief" didn't seem right. I think she did the right thing rescuing the horses. I think the horses agreed. When the neighbors actually sued the Kennedys for horse stealing, my friend's father did some research for the legal team that was assembled to help prepare the Kennedys' defense.

Ethel Kennedy received a not-guilty verdict, so the team of attorneys who successfully defended her got a post-trial surprise. The

Kennedys hosted a victory dinner to thank everyone who had helped with the case. My friend Tommy's dad invited me to go and drove me the twenty-five miles to Hickory Hill, the Kennedys' estate in McLean, Virginia. My heart began beating a little faster as the mansion came into view.

The house looked like the kind of place where servants would serve food and clean up. Maybe they would be black. Servants were almost always black. Perhaps they would let me look them in the eyes. Maybe they would invite me into their lives. As I recall, they stood near the doorways with white gloves on and were extremely friendly. When our car came to a stop and I got out, Ethel Kennedy was there to meet me in a beautiful dress, almost like a formal gown. I know it wasn't a formal dinner, but then these were the Kennedys, and I had put Ethel up there with royalty. I was wearing a coat and tie. In those days I wore a coat and tie to school at St. Stephens School for Boys, an Episcopalian high school in Alexandria, and this was a lot bigger deal than attending classes.

Growing up in Alexandria I'd seen plenty of big homes—George Washington's Mount Vernon, Robert E. Lee's Custis Lee Mansion, the White House, etc.—but my view of mansions until that day was always from afar. The Kennedy home was the biggest house I'd ever been in. I wondered how high the ceilings were. I wondered how many rooms the massive place had. I thought about trying to sneak away to look in every room. Were there twenty, thirty, fifty rooms?

I was directed to the formal dinning room, where I met Senator Kennedy. I was so nervous I just knew I would blurt out something foolish and end any chance I had of being Bobby's friend. I wanted to tell him about almost touching his brother the President a week before he died or that I had seen and heard Dr. King's speech and thought they would get along. Instead I just smiled and said nothing.

The Senator welcomed me warmly with a handshake. It seemed like, felt like, the handshake of someone running for president. Shaking his hand was even more special because I had missed President Kennedy's hand back when I was in the greeting line that day a few years earlier at the White House.

I immediately mentally compared the Kennedy brothers. Robert was smaller than John. He wasn't quite as handsome. He wasn't quite as heroic. Still, I knew he was important. My father knew him in a casually professional way. Even to this day, I count the letters the two exchanged in official correspondence as prized possessions.

Tragically, Robert Kennedy would all too soon meet the same fate as his older brother John, death at the hands of a gunman. If only I could have known the future and warned him, telling him not to run for president, not to follow his fallen brother! I was mesmerized, obviously unaware that in two short years Robert Kennedy's life would be cut short during his campaign for the Democratic nomination for president in 1968. Following a speech in Los Angeles, Sirhan Sirhan would shoot him down. Television cameras captured the horrible event as the nation watched a second Kennedy die.

Any public death is horrifying, especially a public execution. When our heroes are the objects of murder it is distressing beyond words. In my formal religious Episcopalian mind it seemed the Kennedy brothers and Dr. King somehow were pointing back in time to the bravest hero of all who gave his life willingly in an obscure corner of the world and forgotten moment of history. Like theirs, Jesus' blood flowed publicly. His heart broke wide open, and out came a powerful everlasting life.

Maybe John's, Robert's and Martin's deaths would help each of us live better lives. Maybe the power to do what's right for poor people, lost people, disinherited people really flows from the broken hearts of those who give everything. No greater love has anyone than to lay down his life for his friends. *Could it be that the seeming loss of visions is what indeed opens the door for them to come true?* Maybe the lesson I was learning in the midst of all these broken hearts was that true love costs you everything.

Robert Kennedy was full of life when he invited me to take a seat at the large table. I was seated next to Sergeant Shriver, a name that would mean more to me later. My school friend was seated on the other side of the table and at the same moment we noticed someone sitting next to Ethel. Kathleen Kennedy was stunning. I'd never seen a girl so beautiful. She looked like a movie star. She was fifteen, and when you're a fourteen-year-old with raging hormones, it doesn't get much better than that. Oh yeah, it could have gotten a lot better than that, but it became obvious pretty fast that Kathleen had no interest in me or my friend. My attention was therefore frustratingly turned to something else.

Gold-plated flatware. I picked up the knife. It felt good in my hand. I thought it would feel even better in my sport coat pocket. Yes, I thought about stealing from the Kennedys. What would be a better souvenir than a piece of Kennedy silverware? I'd have proof I was there if any doubted my story. Besides, my mom would be very interested in the kind of cutlery Ethel Kennedy preferred. Remembering the handful of souvenir grass from the rose garden lawn under President Kennedy's foot at the White House, I thought this would just add to my collection. On second thought, taking the table knife would certainly get me into deep trouble at Hickory Hill and at home. What if one of the other dinner guests or the servants saw me? At that moment something else caught my eye.

There in the middle of the Kennedys' dinner party was a gigantic

African tortoise. The massive turtle was wandering around in the adjoining room. The Kennedy pet had free range of the house. I followed his slow moving journey during dinner and eventually he meandered outside toward the swimming pool area. The unexpected tortoise was a good preview for what came after dinner.

"Ethel, let's show everyone the pictures from the family vacation," Robert Kennedy announced. He then excused himself, and I didn't see him again. Thinking we would pass around a photo album the guests were shocked when instead he brought out their 16mm projector. A large screen was put in place near the head of the table, and a film began. The Kennedys' home movies looked like a *National Geographic* television special, Robert and Ethel and their eleven children playing on the plains of Africa.

There was footage of them on safari with lions, giraffes, gorillas and birds with feathers brighter than the sun. And there they were, the Kennedys with Africans. These people had skin the color of midnight. Each one was dark black, darker black than any people I'd ever seen.

I wondered what it would be like to go on a vacation to Africa, to a place with people who looked like the broken but determined man walking in my imagination. Our usual vacation spot was Williamsburg, Virginia, but God in his providence knew one day I would indeed go to Africa. Not on vacation, but to change my life. In some ways God planted a seed that night at the Kennedys' that years later would grow and flower into the full harvest of a lifestyle.

CAPE TOWN

Flashing forward twenty-three years, I recall my first time in Africa. The cruel apartheid of South Africa's Cape District was clear to me as I entered the city in the spring of 1989. I came to Cape Town as a singer helping a friend minister to the poor who were packed into local townships like New Yorkers on a subway train. These camp cities were suffocating and life threatening.

Right in the middle of it all, St. James Church, a prominent Cape Town congregation under the leadership of Bishop Frank Retief, had penetrated the poorest township near Cape Town, known as Khayelitsha. The church later suffered a horrible massacre as the result of its efforts for racial reconciliation. We were there working alongside local St. James missionaries who had built a small daycare center in the midst of this million-person refugee camp.

No matter how many times you see scenes like this on television, it can't compare to witnessing it firsthand. But to be in the definite minority was once again thrilling, like the King march, or one day landing in Port-au-Prince, Haiti—a sea of black faces pressing in on me, with that familiar look in the eyes of all those strangers.

I breathed deep the hot air of the African days and nights and looked deep into the dark, almond-brown eyes of my new African friends. To really greet them and look them in their eyes meant things were changing. Changing for me at least and I hope for them. Change is slow; people change, but not much.

Three weeks in South Africa gave me a new understanding of just how poorly we all do at getting along. The times dictated to us that staying where we were was not possible. The President, The Preacher, The Senator were all dead, and their loss just swept us away. However the leader of these black people, Nelson Mandela, was not dead; he was in prison and had been for thirty-plus years. His emergence on the world's stage later in life and his release from jail marked the decline of apartheid as the official policy of South Africa. Unfortunately the unofficial discrimination based on race and color goes on even today.

The disinherited are the broken-hearted ones cut off from their rightful place. They are orphaned with no fame, no fortune, and no future. They are invisible, clouded over by a myth that somehow they are not important.

Understanding that, Dr. Martin Luther King Jr. devoted his life and resources to change the plight of the poor. He used his position of power to expose evil. His fame was easy to discern. I'd seen pictures of him with President Kennedy. I saw him marching on television and talking to reporters about the injustices suffered by black people in America. I remembered his speech at the Lincoln Memorial in Washington. I found myself wanting to be like him. Maybe I could follow his lead and be there for brokenhearted people.

I sometimes wondered how I was different, besides in skin color, from this man who seemed to reach out everywhere, like a giant bird harboring wounded chicks. It sounds remarkable, but I didn't really know anyone who didn't look like me. There had been a few black maids in our home over the years but I never really interacted with them. They passed through the house hardly noticed, silent and efficient.

Robert and Ethel Kennedy were encouraging and inviting as they modeled serving the poor. They, the poor, were included in the Kennedys' circle of influence. God was planting seeds of reneighboring in my heart through these experiences of empowerment and reconciliation.

We moved from Virginia to Michigan as my father relocated our family to the northwest suburbs of Detroit. I had no idea how my life was about to change.

3   Michigan

AFTER THE ASSASSINATION OF ROBERT KENNEDY IN 1968, Hubert Humphrey became the Democratic nominee for president, while Richard Nixon won the Republican nomination. As a loyal Democrat, my father had very little regard for Nixon. Kennedy's close victory over him in 1960 was a great relief for my dad. When Nixon won the election we were already gone from Washington.

Dad was an expert in patent and trademark law. He held two engineering degrees, one from the University of Missouri and the other from Michigan Technological University, and a law degree from the University of Denver Law School. To me, he was one of the greatest attorneys in America and the best dad a boy could have. I wasn't surprised when he was offered an executive position in the legal department of the large automotive supply company Eaton, Yale and Towne.

So, with my father's Washington, D.C., practice slowing and his health beginning to fail, we packed up. I remember the day Dad told us we would be moving to Michigan. My mind rushed back eleven years earlier, the last time my brother and I left Alexandria and the first time I could remember my young heart being wounded.

"Wake up, Sandy; we're going on a trip." My mother called me Sandy. It was a special name of affection she gave me at birth. Mom and Dad were splitting up; I was four years old. Pregnant with her fourth child, Mother put my brother, sister and me in the family station wagon in the middle of the night and drove for two days to Columbia, Missouri, where we would stay with close relatives. I remember wondering, *Where are we going? And why isn't Dad driving?*

My parents eventually did divorce, with an ugly custody battle raging on for a couple of years. The heartache that came from a divided family crushed my mother, Joan, and my two sisters, Laurie and Beth. It also followed my brother and me as we were court-ordered back to Virginia. That was why leaving again now was so hard. My father had remarried a wonderful woman named Millie, my stepmom, and the circumstances seemed better, but there were wounds that went so deep it seemed as if they could never be repaired.

A divided family hurts. Healing can come, but it's not easy. It has affected me and is the foundational part of my brokenness and dysfunction. Formative parts of our lives sometimes are cruel, unexpected and confusing, just as the disruptive divorce forced my flight from home and return to it. God does understand the difficulties of marriage. The apostle Paul reminds us that Christ is wed to us. Whenever I wonder if Jesus really cares about the stress in my relationship with my wife, the answer is always yes. He knows about a tough marriage; he is married to me with all my rebellion and unfaithfulness to him.

Bloomfield Hills, Michigan, is one of the richest cities in America. We ended up moving into a beautiful home there in a safe neighborhood, and my dad went to work every day in Detroit. One of his last assignments was developing the safety device known as the airbag, a standard feature on all cars today.

Automotive technology was intensely competitive, but the Detroit carmakers weren't the only ones under pressure. Race relations were at a boiling point in 1967. Black Americans were tired of the injustice and weary of the struggle for equal rights. The voice of their champion had been silenced. John F. Kennedy was dead. And in Cartown both black people and white people would soon die. The disinherited decided to take matters into their own hands.

The worst race riot in the history of the United States took place in Detroit, Michigan, in the summer of 1967. It all happened twelve miles from my beautiful home where all my neighbors were white. I watched the images on television of angry black men hurling bricks at an army of police. As tension escalated, the National Guard was brought in. There in living color were tanks rolling through the streets of Motor City.

As I viewed the horrifying scenes with my dad on television he said, "It's like they're playing cowboys and Africans," his own racialized way of describing the horror. When it was over forty-three people had died. Blacks and whites bled in the streets, and their blood ran together in one of the darkest days of our nation's history. The view of it in my memory is vivid, since local television stations captured the violence. It reminded me of pictures from early in the civil rights struggle, only instead of water hoses there were tanks, and German shepherds were replaced by fully armed soldiers.

THE ANDOVER REVIVAL

After the riot in the fall of '67, I started my sophomore year at Andover High School. Life in Bloomfield Hills was abundant and free. Everything seemed in place. I was becoming a good football player as a quarterback, with my brother Jeff playing wide receiver. We were a winning team. Though the riots had stirred deep concern, they were receding into the background. The difficulties and pain had left their scars, and my attitude toward life, though optimistic, still reflected a deep need for healing.

In October, a young man named Ray Husband from The Voice of Christian Youth (a part of Youth for Christ) invited me to come to one of their meetings. It sounded interesting and, since many of my friends were also invited, I went. As he shared his faith and asked us our responses to the claims of Christ, something inside me awakened. I know now it was the Holy Spirit drawing me to the Lord. I loved the many conversations that ensued between Ray and me. Ironically, our habit was to meet and talk at the local Howard Johnson's Restaurant, continuing to connect my past with my present. I was converted to Christianity soon after that as the love of Jesus consumed me.

I was anxious to tell my dad of my conversion, and he was very open to my newfound faith. He didn't speak often about his faith, but I was confident he was a believer.

ELATION AND TRAGEDY

It wasn't long before I discovered the most attractive girl at school. I'd admired her ever since we moved to Michigan but never had the guts to ask her out. One day her brother stopped me in the hall at school and said, "When are you going to talk to my sister? She tells stories at the dinner table about you all the time." That's all the convincing I needed. I called her up and asked her if she would like to go to the movies with me. She said yes, and on Saturday night we were off.

As I left the house that April evening for my first date with her, my dad said, "I hear you're going out with that pretty blonde; you know she's a millionaire's daughter!" My excitement was obvious as I instantly replied, "Yes!" Dad said, "Be careful and treat her right. I understand she's special."

I picked her up, and we went to see the Cliff Robertson film *Charlie*. The movie was OK, but sitting next to her felt perfect, and I was numbed by the thrill of it all. After the picture we drove to her home, and I walked her to the front door. I awkwardly kissed her goodnight and asked her if she would go to the spring prom with me. It was the first time I'd kissed a girl. At seventeen I was a slow starter. She said yes and I was sky high. What a night! I was happier than I'd ever been. It was like my whole world was coming together, and I thought it just couldn't get any better. I had my first kiss from the most beautiful and popular girl I'd ever seen. My parents were proud, my friends were happy for me. All the guys would be jealous. It was like I won the Super Bowl!

I couldn't wait to get home and tell my mom and dad the great news. When I walked in the door, my mom was on the couch crying. Her best friend was sitting next to her. She said, "Scott, come here and sit down. I've got to talk to you." She put her hands on me and said, "I'm so sorry, but tonight your dad had a heart attack and didn't make it."

The best day of my life became the worst. My heart shattered. I loved my father, and now he was gone. Suddenly everything appeared to be in slow motion. I left the living room and drifted into his library. My father loved American history, especially the Civil War. The shelves were full of books about Lincoln and Lee and Jackson. I smelled the aging, leather-bound collections. The distinctive scent of my father permeated the room—his pipe, lingering smoke, even his after-shave.

In my brokenness, I cried out a simple prayer to God, "Now that he's gone, you have to be my Father!" In that moment Christianity became so much more than my conversion into a young people's movement. This was real life. I needed God to be there more than ever, though it was hard to believe in a God who would allow my parents to divorce or heroes to die, especially one like my dad. Lord, I believe, help my unbelief. Even with my wonderful stepmother, Millie, I still couldn't shake the feeling of being orphaned, being disinherited and losing a parent.

THE AFRICAN AMERICAN CHURCH

One of my closest Christian brothers was Howard Tryon. He invited me with some others to go with him to a big church in Detroit. We agreed, and so one Sunday morning we headed to the city with his family's African American maid. It was her church. Approaching the house of worship, I mentally compared this neighborhood of tightly packed clapboard houses, most in need of a fresh coat of paint, with mine.

I think my friends and I were the only white people in the huge congregation. The pulpit looked like it was at least two football fields away. There was excitement in the air and the buzz of people laughing and talking and greeting one another with "How've you been? It's so good to see you." I remember the sounds of the Hammond B 3 organ rolling back to where we were. We walked up the center aisle and sheepishly took a seat in a pew in the middle of the sanctuary. The church was filling up, bursting with anticipation.

By the time the preacher started the service, the place was packed and buzzing with voices of friends catching up with each other. And it was all about to get louder. Everywhere I had attended church everyone became quiet when the preacher got up. Not here. The organ music got more intense, and shouts of "Thank you, Lord!" and "Praise your name, Jesus!" reverberated all around us. And then there were the tambourines. They were everywhere, raised in the air as the tiny attached cymbals rattled with the spinning of the hand.

The preacher opened the service with prayer. You could hear him pray through the excitement. All around me I heard "Amen!" "That's right!" and "Bless you, Lord!" When he finished his prayer, another man got up and led the church in a song. It seemed that the room temperature rose. I remember the beautiful voices and how I could hear the joy in their singing. Hands were clapping and the tambourines were now keeping perfect rhythm. I was an Episcopalian, I thought, and we worshiped God in quiet and in order. This was loud and I loved it. It was my first time in a black church. Somewhere deep inside I vowed it wouldn't be my last.

It reminded me of the sights and sounds of that summer day years earlier in Washington, D.C., listening to Dr. Martin Luther King Jr. Now was a time of growing up and a time of realization. Could this comfort be connected to the providential way God works with disinherited feelings? Was I comforted and challenged by a black church willing to accept me while I remained in a culture unwilling to welcome them? Would it change me? Would I allow it to?

So, in that sense, I did grow up in the wealthy white suburbs of Detroit, ironically the home of the now famous Motown Records. To this day it may be the coolest record company in music history. The president and founder of Motown, Berry Gordy, discovered and produced records for dozens of stars from "Little Stevie" Wonder to Diana Ross and the Supremes to The Temptations.

You could always see three or four groups at a time by catching concerts put on by Gordy called "Motown Reviews." I went to a few of those shows with some friends who loved soul music. One night at a review in Pontiac Central High School's football stadium I saw Little Anthony and the Imperials and The Temptations. We sang along to "Tears on My Pillow" and "My Girl." The music was great, and the dancing moves incredible. Just like at Howard's maid's church, if there were any other white guys there that night I didn't see them, but we were comfortable. We weren't afraid and had no reason to be. I loved the music, and my love for the people was growing. I remember the anthem popularized by James Brown, "Say it loud, I'm black, I'm proud!" We joined in enthusiastically—all those around us welcomed us.

GIVE HIM YOUR PANTS

As a result of a successful high school football career, I was offered a scholarship to DePauw University in Greencastle, Indiana. I liked college life. I went to class in the morning and spent the afternoons at football practice. The games were fun and I had some success, though our team was not good, and there were no scouts from the NFL coming to see us. DePauw wasn't exactly a "pro player" producing school.

As a member of the DePauw Tigers' traveling squad and the second string halfback, I often missed my dad's encouragement and presence in my life, wishing he could come and watch me play. He had been a college football player and so was my brother Jeff. We had learned the game from Dad. It was a way of life for us from the time we were little.

Football afforded me an opportunity to spend time on the road with my roommate, Lester Woods, our starting tailback. He was a great athlete and my closest African American friend. During one game, Lester was carrying the ball around our right end while our head coach, Tommy Mont, urged him on. As he was tackled and carried out of bounds, he tore his game pants. Immediately the coach yelled, "Roley!" and I jumped off the bench enthusiastically with my helmet in hand and replied, "Yes Sir!" I was ready to go in the game and take Lester's place. This was my big chance! My girlfriend was in the stands.

At that moment the coach turned to Lester and, seeing the ripped pants, whirled around to me in front of everyone and commanded "Roley, give him your pants!" My coach literally expected me to peel off my game pants, taking me down to only a jock and my girdle pads, in front of everyone. It was the most humiliating moment of my football career. Fortunately for me, when Lester tore his pants he also injured his knee. So instead of stripping off my pants, I got to go in and play. I was redeemed!

Not long after this incident I also blew out my knee. The injury eventually forced me out of football.

At DePauw I had a few friends who were members of the radical group Students for a Democratic Society (SDS). The establishment called them radicals and militants, and in a very real way they were. They did many violent things to try to get their message out. In the late 1960s, the chapter at DePauw blew up the ROTC building to protest the war in Vietnam. As the war escalated into Laos and Cambodia in 1972, the SDS chapter at DePauw organized a school-wide boycott of all final exams. I wasn't a card-carrying member of the SDS, but did decide to join in the boycott. Four hundred of the twenty-five hundred students at DePauw participated. Leadership in the SDS reasoned that boycotting final exams would force the university to close down and appeal to the federal government to change its foreign policy. It didn't work the way they hoped, but it did cause a major headache for the school.

The chancellor allowed the students to make up the exams. I was stubborn. I believed in the cause. I stood my ground while 399 of 400 returned to take their exams. I was the lone holdout. I dropped out. I didn't graduate, and I didn't really care. It was about so much more than the war in Vietnam for me. It was the battle for my heart and soul. My emotions were ravaged. I lost my family to divorce, my dad to a heart attack, and now because of an injury, football was gone along with my education. At least I still had Jesus. But I couldn't feel his arms around me. I couldn't feel his heartbeat. My brokenness was like a prison cell holding my damaged emotion. I needed healing.

BACK TO MICHIGAN

I retreated to Michigan to lick my wounds. I couldn't go back to De-Pauw. I was still on track to graduate with my degree in philosophy, but the shame of the failed boycott made returning impossible. I spent time with old friends. I had some good talks with them and the brother who led me to the Lord. He listened to me and prayed with me and told me about a Christian college not far from my mother's Michigan home. I decided to transfer in the fall. Little did I know that taking refuge to find some peace would lead me to the place where I would find myself through music and meet the girl I would marry.

What was awakened in me as a youngster became amplified as an adolescent. My parents' divorce and my father's untimely death produced a haunting sense of loss which can never really be articulated or recovered—an early identification with those who were hurting, especially those souls who seemed ravaged by society. I remembered the liquid eyes of my housekeeper, the wandering black man and featureless faces hidden from me only because I was too fearful to look.

My desire to connect, somehow, endured because I trusted Dr. King, who reminded us we needed one another. He called a nation to follow and then bravely led the way. I also remembered the overwhelming feeling of privilege, dining with the Kennedys even as powerless servants watched in white gloves.

I later realized that the streets of Detroit were not very different from the apartheid-ruled streets of South Africa, though military tanks and soldiers had blocked our view of an emerging black cultural revolution demonstrated by dancing on the sidewalk to Motown's captivating soulful rhythms and pre-hip-hop sounds.

The country club life I had lived was being brought under the microscope of reality. I was being challenged to review what had been force-fed me and then somehow change that diet to feed a hungry heart ready again to be broken—just like my newfound faith was teaching me had happened to my Lord, the greatest lover of all. Maybe the God I served was calling me to follow in the same way Martin Luther King Jr. had. Maybe God was showing me that my heart had to be exposed enough to be shattered but resilient enough so that in brokenness it could find the life it longed for: a complete life, a full life, an abundant life.

Christ's broken heart on the cross two thousand years ago comforted the brokenness in my life. I watched four heroes die unexpectedly: Martin Luther King Jr., John F. Kennedy, Robert Kennedy and the deepest loss, my father. I was hurt and felt like dying myself. Jesus had been hurt and then died to prove his love. I realized his return from the grave was the good news of the gospel. He was indeed alive, and by faith I was united to him.

Freedom was always the goal, individually and corporately. It was being redefined for me as a living power that led me to do what was right. My own broken heart taught me that I couldn't begin to imagine the freedom I could obtain simply by letting go of my own bias, myths of supremacy and plain old bad ideas. Real freedom to embrace selfless love for the brokenhearted required me to love each wounded person from my own broken heart.

Ray Husband was the young man who shared Christ with me when I was in high school. He was now the director of admissions at Spring Arbor College. It was a small Christian school near Jackson, Michigan, and he encouraged me to transfer. That sounded good, but what really sealed the deal was that my brother Jeff was also transferring to Spring Arbor from the University of Missouri where he had been a student athlete and football player the past three years.

It was great being back with my brother. His young heart had also been broken over the loss of our father, and the love we shared was growing stronger. When he arrived on campus he brought his drum set with him. We played music together and basically rediscovered a deep friendship and brotherhood shattered by pain but now resurrected by love.

Our abrupt relocations, moves from northern Virginia to Michigan, then from college to college, drifting and wandering, were displacements. We were chasing mirages that looked inviting but never fully satisfied. I continued my philosophy studies at Spring Arbor and added classes in African American history and sociology. I plunged into my studies with zeal hoping to understand better the most dispersed people group on the planet.

LINDA RAE KENDALL

"I've got someone I want you to meet," were the first words Ray said to me as I arrived on Spring Arbor College's campus in the fall of 1972. My friend told me that she was a singer and that the two of us would make a good match because of our musical interests.

As a student representative, Linda Rae Kendall was waiting for us across campus in front of the Science Center, directing bewildered students to orientation tables. She had kind eyes and was really cute. Though I sensed she had a good heart, what I most remember was her perfect, long blonde hair with collegiate knee socks. When she laughed, her bright green eyes disappeared like closing doors leaving only her smile.

As I introduced myself, the words of my friend still clogged my ears. Just moments before while we were crossing campus to finally meet her he had said, "Pay attention, Scott, I might be introducing you to the next Mrs. Roley." We went on our first date one month later. It was September 1972. For the next eighteen months we played music, studied, talked about our dreams and fell in love. She came from a wonderful Christian family and was everything I was looking for in a girl. We committed our lives to one another and somehow knew we'd be together.

I was a first semester senior at Spring Arbor College majoring in philosophy, but after a dispute with one of my professors I decided there were better things to do. A sociology class which paid a visit to the Chicago-based ministry of the Reverend Jesse Jackson and his Operation PUSH (People United to Save Humanity) headquarters had shown me the need for being on the streets. One way of doing that was as a singer. I had music to make and worlds to seek.

In January of 1974 I got a job performing in Holiday Inn lounges. It paid a humble salary of $190 a week plus room and board. I was a professional musician, was improving on the guitar and could play songs by Jim Croce, Cat Stevens and James Taylor. I started writing my own songs and once in a while I'd sing an original tune between "Morning Has Broken" and "You've Got a Friend."

As a young Christian I was still searching for my musical soul. I loved the music of Woody Guthrie. He used it to effect change. He chronicled the plight of poor families who fled the Dust Bowl of Oklahoma in the 1930s for the promised land of California, only to find life often worse there, living in tent cities working as migrant farm hands. He sang about the struggle for "the pickers" to unionize and so much more.

Guthrie also wrote the classic song that praises the beauty of our Lord's creation, "This land is your land, this land is my land, . . . from the redwood forests to the Gulf Stream waters . . . this land was made for you and me." Somehow in my pursuit of freedom and truth, this land seemed made more for some and less for others. Guthrie cried out about social injustice. Woody cared about the poor. He *was* changing the world with his music. I wanted to do that too.

I wanted to see the America Guthrie sang about. I wanted to go places I'd never been. So I did. I stuck out my thumb and got in the first car that stopped. My hitchhiking included trips to California, Canada, Mexico and the marvelous Rocky Mountains. Sometimes I rode freight trains without an invitation. My friend Steve Vanker and I hopped a train in Sacramento and rode it all the way to Salt Lake City, Utah. I also traveled across Canada. I rode a train from Montreal, Quebec, to Thunder Bay, Ontario, with college roommate Ron Kopicko. It was fun. It was daring, but experiencing the beauty of the land from a box car door or an engineer's window was the best. Too much freedom from responsibility was changing me. I needed direction, so I headed home. I returned to Michigan and saw my relationship with Linda developing into a life partnership. I ended my wandering, and we decided to marry.

We settled in the working-class suburbs of Detroit. The rented houses we lived in were a far cry from Alexandria's Old Town or Bloomfield Hills. We may not have been living a life of poverty, but it was close. We weren't in the ghetto but you could see it from the bedroom window. We were on a mission field and didn't know it.

Linda finished her time at Spring Arbor working on a degree in special education. She was offered a job with the state's social services, caring for severely mentally and physically impaired children. I still have a vivid image in my mind of one young boy named Jimmy. He had neither arms nor legs. Linda brought him to our home. I will never forget his smile. He knew he was loved.

I admired the true heart of compassion Linda had. If King and Kennedy planted the seed of compassion in me, I now saw firsthand what it looked like for love to flower through Linda. She modeled for me what I saw in another hero, Mother Teresa of Calcutta.

Mother Teresa gave her life away and cared for dying patients, people overlooked by Indian society and deemed unworthy to live. Linda and I experienced that firsthand as we traveled through India on a missions trip in the fall of 2003. It may have been in a different context. The children Linda cared for were not in the Third World, but the spirit was the same—true loving care for those who, for reasons known only to God, really needed help.

Linda gave freely. Her love watered the seed King and Kennedy planted in my heart. My fractured soul opened up a little bit more. Her healing words were, "If you're going to love, you will love others because you've been loved so well." It was the overflow of grace and mercy. Could it be that God was showing me the truth through Linda's needy and forgotten kids? Jesus said they were worth dying for. The world said they were to be thrown away.

4   Tennessee

MY JOURNEY INTO MUSIC BEGAN WITH MY FATHER AND mother's love for the arts. Mom had been a dancer schooled in ballet and an opera-trained vocalist. She performed a classic song and dance for us kids as she prepared our meals, beginning subtly and slowly, then reaching a grand crescendo, always finishing with a perfect presentation of this week's pot roast and some obscure aria.

The obnoxious sounds and dated songs were unmistakably my father's, and from my bedroom under any pillow I could find, the rationalization of murdering him or escape by suicide kept prodding me through his loud, out-of-tune voice. His favorite, "Waltzing Matilda," floated upstairs to my boyhood bedroom like the first black cloud rising from a house fire. All I could do was roll over and surrender in the face of such a daunting task as trying to make him stop.

For me, music had to do with wrestling a cornet in the elementary school band and a $15 pawnshop Harmony guitar my father bought me when I was twelve years old. I thought it was a nice gift. The Beatles were my favorite group, and I wanted to be like Paul McCartney. I can remember the Beatles' first concert in Washington, D.C., at the

Capital Arena on a revolving stage. I wanted to go, but my parents felt it would be too dangerous. That of course added to the mystique of making music for a living.

FROM MOTOR CITY TO MUSIC CITY

The lure of music drew me in, and over the next decade I saw more and more how I could be happy living my life as a rock 'n' roll star. I must admit the secondhand guitar didn't get a lot of use at first. I'd pull it out and play it once in a while, pretending to be Paul. As a sixth grader and beyond, I was more interested in sports, so it was ironic that sports brought the guitar back into my life ten years later. I tore the cartilage in my left knee playing football at DePauw University and later in that year returned to Michigan for surgery. During my rehab I picked the guitar back up and never really put it down. As I was dropping out of school, traveling and making my attempt to be a "wanderer poet," I made a move.

Music continued to be the center of my life. I acted on the talent I had and kept working hard to build a career. The Lord brought a couple of other musicians into my life who helped me rise to the next level. Mike Albrecht was a friend from high school. He had a beautiful, inviting voice and was a unique guitar player. He played an S-model Martin D-35 guitar, the Cadillac of stringed instruments. Alan Moore also played a Martin. His voice had a fragile quality, and he could sing high. He was a skilled bass player and wrote great songs. We discovered that our voices blended well, and Albrecht, Roley and Moore was born.

We recorded our debut album at Tri-Art studios in Bismarck, North Dakota, on the banks of the Missouri River. Bismarck is not exactly a music business mecca, but the studio was affordable, and so was our producer. Greg Nelson would come to fame later in Nash-

Albrecht, Roley and Moore, 1975. Mike Albrecht, Scott Roley and Al Moore.

ville, making records for Sandi Patti, Larnell Harris, Steve Green and many others. He helped us sound good in the studio, and his string arrangements were full and beautiful.

AR&M wrote all the songs on the album, and "Gently Flowing Feeling" was chosen as the title track. James Isaac Elliott was our mandolin player, and he took the photograph of the three of us that ended up as the album's front cover. James's own songs have now far outdistanced mine in popularity. He and I are to this day a musical team. James remains my instructor and professor, not only in songwriting but in life as well.

One of the promoters we did concerts with in Indiana had moved to Nashville to form a management and booking company. He liked our music, and we asked him to manage our group. He sent our album to Billy Ray Hearn, who had recently launched a new label called Spirit Records. Hearn founded Sparrow Records in 1975. After we had toured with Keith Green, Second Chapter of Acts and the Talbot Brothers, Billy Ray signed our group to his new label. We moved from Detroit to Nashville in the summer of 1978 to record our second album, *Starlighter*, the first for the Spirit label.

I loved Nashville. I still do. It's a big small town or a small big town depending on your view. I hadn't exactly "made it" in Christian music but I was living in Music City, I had a record deal, Linda had given birth to our first child, Matthew, and we were recording with two of the hottest producers in town. My music was reaching only a small audience, but many of my listeners were socially minded people with an agenda of caring for the poor, hoping to make a difference in the world.

WITHIN MY REACH

As I chased my dream, it always was just out of reach. Later God taught me who *was* within my reach: the hurting, the lost, the poor, and the underserved. There were enough good things happening with our music careers to keep us looking for the gold, but we never hit the mother lode.

Perhaps the band was slowed by my mixed motives. On one hand I wanted to do something to help others, as Mother Teresa, King and the Kennedys had taught me. I wanted to be like Woody Guthrie. On the other hand I wanted to be a star. I wanted to sell a million records and perform before thousands. It may be possible for some to do both, but not for me. My limited talent stalled my progress in the music business, and my need to serve was accelerating the call to pastoral community development and missional living.

It's a narrow road that leads to heaven. I was on my way to heaven but traveling a wide road, from Michigan to Florida and Tennessee to California. So the call to settle in Nashville in the late '70s became for me the discovery of an oasis. The pursuits of music, love, adventure, and true purpose were the excuses that led me there. What was real food and real drink and true rest for my soul came simply in the power to do the right thing.

I was living a wild, self-centered life for most of those early years. I didn't go to church very often. Though Linda came from a very churched family, we just didn't feel the need to go. I hadn't found Jesus in church and didn't see its importance. We had tried attending a few churches in Nashville, but we didn't fit in. They were mostly traditional churches, from which I proudly and foolishly distanced myself, even though I came from faint Episcopalian and Presbyterian roots. I was a proud convert from a nontraditional background. I was led to Christ through a parachurch ministry and much influenced by the Jesus movement, yet I even refused to go to those types of churches. I was simply rebellious. The power to do the right thing comes from love, Christ's love.

One night after listening to me perform in Dallas, Texas, a black woman said, "You just love the world too much." She was older, more conservative and a true mother of the church. I was convicted by her words. She reminded me of Mother Teresa, King, the Kennedys and my dad. She helped me accept social justice as important to God. Renewal in my heart could only be accomplished through faith in Christ. I needed the church to help me past an individualized lifestyle caring less about pain in others and more about protecting myself. My dilemma seemed to be summed up in a simple question: Where would I find a true expression of Christ's church that would actually welcome and take in the likes of me?

Scotty Smith and Michael Card

Linda and my brother Jeff were most helpful in answering that question. As advocates for the poor and people with strong faith in Christ,

I trusted them. We leaned against each other in a small community, holding up against the strong breezes blowing, threatening to destroy us. The threats included pride, unbelief, and other temptations— stealing, lying, cheating, overeating. You name it, we were infected with it.

These destructive winds changed unexpectedly in the spring of 1978. My band, Albrecht, Roley and Moore, played in downtown Winston-Salem, North Carolina, which continually smelled like fresh-cut tobacco. Our promoter, Scott Ward Smith, and I sat in the parlor of his church and talked about all of these various struggles. We discussed the problems of brokenness, inequality for the poor, and the dream of Martin Luther King's Mountaintop of Hope. Mostly we talked about Redskins football and North Carolina basketball.

We also dreamed about a day when two foolish men might start a church where broken people could gather and be healed by Jesus. We would live in community through all the fear, foolishness, inconsistency, hatred, rebellion and lost love. That night after the concert AR&M packed the van to head out, and I took one last long draw of the tobacco-rich atmosphere of Winston-Salem, hoping in Jesus those dreams would come true.

To earn extra money, I did studio work singing on commercials. One of AR&M's record producers also contracted singers to do jingles. Sometimes he would hire me to sing. I met Michael Card as we were being crammed into a small vocal booth to sing on a commercial for a local Nashville bank.

Mike Card was a real person who was doing what I wanted to do. His recognizable name, lifestyle and integrity made me want to be like him and to be with him. I had no idea that singing trite phrases about "saving accounts," "check books" and "safety deposit boxes" would become life-changing, all because of the man singing next to me. Though later in our careers we played a lot of songs together and traveled a bunch of miles, his greatest influence of love and care was not musically. It was as a comrade and brother who would share my desire for community, racial reconciliation and the intentional call to live as Christian men in word and deed!

With some sadness, my big brother Jeff stayed in Michigan. He had his own reconciliation ministry to build. He was helping to save poor kids from Detroit who had no hope of their own. He was with me at the King march, where we both first heard the call to social work. He supported moves toward helping the poor and racial reconciliation for as long as I could remember. He was my drummer, my wide receiver, and the one who had the dream to buy some land and create a boys' ranch. In many ways, what was happening to me in Tennessee resulted from a vision we shared from our view of Martin Luther King Jr.'s speech that our father encouraged us to hear that hot August day so long ago.

My friend from Winston-Salem, Scotty Smith, moved to Nashville in the fall of 1978 to become the youth pastor at First Presbyterian Church. Our friendship blossomed along with the shared vision of community that Michael, Linda, Jeff, James and I continued to pray for. I finally felt like there was a reason to go to church. Our fellowship was enriched by the gospel. God's grace and mercy were at the heart of Scotty Smith's teaching. His mentor, Jack Miller, and Michael Card's mentor, Bill Lane, helped us see our need to be connected.

THE DRUMMER

Several years later, I was in Cincinnati, Ohio, playing a musical concert with my band City Limits. It was a group of very skilled musicians who agreed to play with me on a tour of cities promoting my newly released record entitled *City Limits*. They were all players way over my head, and I was extremely fortunate to have them assembled, making me look and sound good.

The drummer's name was Joe English. He was famous around the world as Paul McCartney's drummer from the band Wings. He had a unique style, playing left-handed behind a right-handed set-up. Joe played hard and loud and creatively. His nickname was "Boom Boom," which fit his playing and personality. He was a big guy who loved music and was always ready to have fun. His drum set, called a *kit,* and drum seat, called a *throne,* were supplied by Tama. English even had handmade graphite drum sticks, which no one was allowed to touch. His drum set was completely off limits.

Joe English was one of the world's best drummers on the industry's best equipment, and, shockingly, he was in my band. A predictable mob of people would come to see Joe play. So we obliged them by finishing every show with his performing a patented Joe English drum solo. It ended in a flurry of arms, cymbals crashing, tom-toms booming, explosions and cheering crowds drowning out everything on stage—closing the evening with each member of the crowd full of joy, smiles, wonder and disbelief. I often characterized my career as "snatching anonymity from the jaws of fame," and the fact that I failed to capitalize on such a promising show explains why that adage came to be my motto.

This particular night all went well. We had a great crowd, enthusiastic and complimentary. Joe was playing great, and by the end of the concert he had the audience right where he wanted them. As he finished his solo, people pressed forward and surrounded the stage area, nearly carrying him off. The evening was coming to a close, and the last of the people were saying their goodbyes, getting their final Joe English autographs, and just lingering maybe to hear a Paul McCartney story or two.

Then a small black child from the audience, around five or six years old, wandered out across the stage. He approached Joe's drum set, and crawled up on the drum throne. The boy picked up the custom-built, sacred graphite sticks, reached out as far as he could, and began banging on anything he could hit. It was a sporadic sound of sticks hitting drum shells, rims, cymbal edges, air. It was indeed some serious noise because the microphones covering the entire drum set were still on, and the sounds came pouring out over the house P.A. system

Joe caught an earful of the little guy imitating him, dismissed himself from some fans, and headed over to his drum set to help the young man find his parents and say good night. What happened next surprised me because I was assuming Joe would whack the boy upside the head or something maybe less punitive, but still designed to stop the unlawful behavior. Instead of disciplining the child, Joe English lifted him up, grabbing the boy's small hands in his with the drum sticks still attached, and then Boom Boom slid his huge frame under the kid as he lifted him onto his legs.

The boy went limp in Joe's grasp, and English just smiled as he took the child through a series of tests. First the snare. Joe lifted the limp boy's right arm up high and then slammed it down on the snare drum, the stick perfectly placed in the center of the drum head. The sound of the cleanly executed snare shot reverberated around the concert hall like someone had fired off a cannon.

The next stop: the set of toms positioned on racks out of the boy's reach above Joe's head. He lifted the boy up and took him through a series of drum licks, hitting each tom-tom again, perfectly. Then Joe added the cymbals, high hat and floor toms. By the time he was done, he had the boy actually playing his entire signature solo reserved for the ending of each show.

As Boom Boom finished playing through the boy, who by this time looked like a limp rag doll, the entire place, still occupied by radio disc jockeys, concert personnel, roadies, musicians and lingering Joe English fans, went crazy. It was his solo all over again, this time played by a small child whose mouth was hanging open with amazement and eyes filled with wonder and joy.

In some obscure way, this illustration helps me better understand the empowerment of disinherited people. The disinherited are cut off from their rightful place. They are not allowed to exist. They are an ignored group that has every right to be here. The disenfranchised are held back from opportunities because of the power of racialization[1] and other dominant culture sin patterns.

The young African American boy moved out of the common crowd to a point on stage reserved for the gifted and the privileged. Instead of being knocked down, the child was allowed a part in creating. His best effort was the noise of imitation. However, in the hands of the expert, maybe a metaphor for the perfect one, Jesus, the young person played music as it was intended. With knowledge and opportunity, the young man was empowered to be the best drummer he could be.

On the other side, of those to whom much is given much is required, and it was to Joe English's credit that he welcomed the chance to share his gift and resources. Just for one night this famous drummer visited a little boy's neighborhood and created a memory that will last a lifetime.

Our God has relocated to earth through Jesus' incarnation, and now his Holy Spirit allows us to share as members of Christ's body in his divine plan. In some way he operates his perfect plan of redemption through us, sinners who deserve death and hell.

Am I surrendered in the hands of the Master Musician, or do I insist on playing by my rules? Do I make real the opportunities for those around me to grow and prosper, or do I hoard the gifts and talents God has given me as if I've earned them and deserve them? Why was I born in America among the upper-middle class, with every privilege and opportunity my family resources could afford? Why was I not born in Haiti or the Sudan, among the poorest of the poor, sick and without resources to find even a simple meal?

God alone has those answers. Our responsibility is to act out of his grace and mercy and to look for opportunities to empower disinherited people. Ironically we get more from those we serve than they receive from us. We are, each of us, at the same time both the powerful drummer and the powerless boy.

As I look back, the two major moves from Virginia to Michigan and Michigan to Tennessee showed me that changing locations didn't stop the turmoil in my heart. You take yourself with you. I had awakened from a slumber to stumble hard into a brokenness only the God of the universe could heal. His method was always to drive me back to himself through the appearances of false summits, partially blocked passageways, and trials that begged me to believe I was safe—when behind their false welcome was the trap of unfulfillment, despair, hatred, and sin.

Could it be that through our small group of weary wanderers a community of brokenhearted fools was indeed becoming a true church? That a broken heart was a common thing and what longing for redemption really pointed to was the search and journey our hearts take together? Maybe God was finally answering the question of why all the unsettled lust for wandering continued to lead me to faces named Linda, Jeff, Mike, James and Scotty. In the end the true resting place was in the heart of Jesus. Whatever our community's best would be, it would only reflect him. The rest, though seemingly beautiful, seductive and appealing, would have to be resisted. The love of Jesus would force it out!

THE NEIGHBORHOOD CRAB

Children on our street referred to her as the neighborhood crab. She was mean-spirited, with an underdeveloped sense of humor and an overdeveloped sense of protection for her front yard—which made it almost life-threatening for any kids to chase family pets or baseballs that accidentally ended up there. My limited contact kept me skeptical of her reputation, assuming the young people were exaggerating.

My son Matthew was a first grader and an all-star Little League baseball player. One day while playing catch with him I overthrew his outstretched arm, and the baseball rolled harmlessly into the neighborhood crab's yard. I motioned Matt to retrieve the ball, and he responded, "Not in this lifetime! Don't you know that's the neighborhood crab's yard?" I wondered why he was so terrified.

I decided to show my six-year-old what a real man looked like when facing his fears, so with the well-faked confidence of an astronaut stepping onto the surface of the moon, I glanced sheepishly at her front picture window and, seeing the coast was clear, entered the yard.

Almost instantly, the neighborhood crab pulled her car around the corner and into her driveway. As she stopped she looked up, and our eyes met. By this time I held the ball in my hand with a guilty look on my face. I had been making my escape from her yard via the sidewalk near where she usually parked her car. She realized the situation and gunned the engine, racing up the driveway toward me, finally screeching to a halt in what seemed to be an attempted murder. I jumped away, clearing the front bumper by inches.

Then as her window came shooting down and her angry face projected out, I came under the fire of her hostile accusations. "What are you doing in my yard?" she shouted. "Are you stealing something? Are you lost? Do you know what trespassing is?"

Overreacting a bit, I screamed at the top of my voice, "Yes, I know what trespassing is. I came into your yard to retrieve my son's baseball, which he would have gladly done had he not been fearful of his life because of your reputation as an ugly-minded woman who lives a pathetic life with nothing better to do than scare little kids!"

She started crying. I was expecting a more volatile and less sympathetic reaction. I walked away shocked at my behavior and especially convicted of my insensitivity, hemming and hawing as I looked into the face of my disbelieving children. What is up with Dad? The question written on tiny faces made the short walk away from her car feel like a mile. Then from behind me like an arrow finding its plump target, the words came staggered within her sobbing, perfectly to my ears, "And you call yourself a Christian?"

Where do you go when you're ready to die? Here were my children, the small but mighty living monuments to my legacy, the future of my seed, staring at me dumbfounded. The truth was I did claim to be a Christian and was so bad at actually sharing Christ's love that though I claimed him, he certainly once again had all the proof he needed to disown me. The gospel is the only answer to why he didn't just kill me then and there. It must be that God truly did allow his Son's death as a substitute for my well-deserved punishment.

The irony of this debacle was that at that moment my daughter Emily came running through our small living room, banging open the front screen door, completely unaware of what was happening, yelling, "Daddy, Daddy, your song's on the radio, your song's on the radio!" For any songwriter, that is indeed a precious moment when your words and music float out over the airwaves searching for potential listeners and record buyers, hoping to communicate the deepest truths of your artist's heart.

This was our family's first opportunity to sit and listen to the single from my newly released album, *Within My Reach.* The title track was the first radio song out. So as I stumbled up the short stairs into the front room of the house, these words greeted me, blasting out of our cheap Pioneer speakers with my smiling proud family standing together cheering me on. It was my music, my voice, my words and it went like this: "We agree that love should be the purpose of the earth, the way you love your neighbor is a measure of your worth." Those opening lines were all I heard.

Hypocrisy is nasty in any form. The sooner we deal with the fact that we are untrustworthy promise breakers, the quicker we find faith in the beautiful trustworthy, promise keeper Jesus. My wife and children and neighbors needed to hear my confession and repentance as I sought their forgiveness for the way I treated our later-to-be friend across the street.

I dismissed myself from the radio show and walked over to apologize to the woman. We ended a cordial several-minute forgiveness-seeking conversation with the idea that I did call myself a Christian and so did she. We were both beggars, and we needed the Bread of Life.

Fortunately my children, the living monuments, got an eyeful and an earful of what we all need to be able to move on: intentional change of heart through faith in the One who has given us a new heart. This is what leads us to love those who are very different from us. Dismantling hypocrisy is our lifelong challenge. It is individual and corporate. As a singer-songwriter I wondered what else might be in store, feeling like a blind man attempting to find in the dark a handle to a doorway that would lead my family and me to truth.

5   Adoption

MY WIFE, LINDA, AND I SHARED A FAMILY PHILOSOPHY THAT went something like this: If there was an empty chair at the dinner table, we should fill it with someone who doesn't have a place to eat. If there was a spare bedroom in the house, we should put someone in it who has no place to sleep. If a child didn't have a mother or father to love her or him, we should become that child's parent, and if there were elderly persons who had no children or family to care for, we should invite them to care for ours. The Roleys have, as a consequence of this philosophy, a lot of aunts, uncles, cousins, sisters, brothers, moms, dads, grandmothers and grandfathers, most of them unrelated by blood but happily related in love.

In a world where so many people are left out of deep, caring relationships it seems the call to Christians is to extend and invite them to be loved. Mahatma Gandhi promoted the idea of adopting the forgotten children of one's enemy. I would say that heeding Jesus' call to love our enemies could be defined as adopting defenseless children and opening our homes to share what we've been given with the forgotten kids of a sometimes cold, cruel and fallen world.

Maybe Jesus' welcoming all of us into a relationship with God and an eternity of living with him should spill out into our welcoming the least and the lost into a relationship with our loved ones for as long as we live on earth.

Foster and adoptive care are two of the simplest and most challenging ways for Christians to engage the poor. Foster care has its ups and downs in that you develop close relationships and ties with people who move on, and it does hurt to let them go. However, the upside, which far outweighs the down, is that when foster children leave they are usually reunited with their natural family, and the feeling of success at that moment is praiseworthy and glorifying to God. Adoptive care is different in that it provides the joy of actually giving your name to a nameless child.

The ministry of adoption and foster care in our family has produced fourteen fantastic foster children and three beautiful adopted kids. When Linda and I agreed to this lifestyle of trying to make our home a "safe house" for children, what we really hoped for was to be effective among the little people who had special needs. At the time we began this work a special needs child was defined as any white child over the age of three and any child of color, meaning a Native American, African American, Hispanic, Asian or mixed-race child. Obviously children with physical, emotional and mental impairments as well as multiple sibling situations fit the category too.

Linda's work among severely mentally impaired children in Michigan early in our marriage helped prepare us for our lifestyle choice to take on foster and adoptive care years later when we moved to Tennessee. The children she ministered to were the neediest of the needy. Some of them she brought home and others she visited in their homes, attempting to reach out beyond simply being their classroom teacher.

This extra effort continued all through our marriage as Linda made sure those around her felt loved. I have learned so much about giving by just watching Linda's natural response to those in need. She would eventually take strong steps to educate our own children through home schooling when necessary and by giving them special tutoring when needed. As an educator she did a remarkable job with our foster, adopted and natural-born children, in spite of living with a husband who was gone a lot and was clearly educationally challenged. I was given the title of headmaster of the "Happy Days Home School" during the time Linda educated our children at home and loved my role teaching history and geography. After all, I'd hitchhiked across most of the United States and Canada. Philosophy and theology were my favorite subjects to teach our little crew!

While I was chasing my musical dreams, Linda continued to reach out to those in need. It was her compassion that brought the first African American to live in our home. Kenya Lashell Currie Franklin was a newborn. While her mother completed a prison sentence at the nearby Tennessee Women's Correctional Institute, we had the privilege of caring for Kenya. Her brown skin, and her mother's black skin, made me remember how afraid and curious I was as a child about those who looked different than me.

These thoughts, and more, directed me to a revival of what I knew was true. I was learning there was much to receive from brothers and sisters of other races. Blacks, browns and the darker hues before had been harsh to me, but now they became inviting. They reflected my healing. I loved baby Kenya. I've come to appreciate her as another piece of the reconciliation puzzle. She would not be the last African American baby to live in our home. The next time a child of a different race would come to us he would not leave in nine months.

The road of empowering the disinherited led us into the world of adoption. The taking in of children who are from minorities or are mixed race is one of the most effective ways to see the gospel demonstrated and empowerment go forward. The adoption of a perceived enemy goes a long way as an action designed to repair broken relationships. It also adds to your heart the joy of falling in love with someone you might never have picked as a son or daughter, mom or dad, sister or brother.

Our future move into an exclusively black neighborhood was in some sense a way to touch our African American heritage. It was something for our whole family to enjoy because in adoption, unlike foster care, you enter into your new family's heritage, and by law it becomes your own. Sam and Jeff, our adopted African American and racially mixed sons, quite literally changed the complexion of our family. I desire now to know more about my African and Hispanic heritage because legally that's where my new family comes from.

The battle to overcome the temptation of thinking that one race is better than another is fought everyday at our breakfast table and every night around our family discussions concerning religion, television, music, movies, violence, drugs, sex, video games, sports and so on. Is there a mutual sort of empowerment going on? Am I the one in need or are these wonderful boys the ones desperate for help?

Bad thinking keeps people away from each other by fabricating fear and doubts. We are told from birth by these myths that differences in folks cannot be overcome. Are there real sacrifices in empowering the disinherited? Absolutely. In fact in our own family we have wrestled deeply over the challenges made to include each of our children as members in the Roley household. Some of us have been hurt, and some of us have done the hurting. We are, however, all in it together. By God's grace and mercy we will survive the pain and anguish to stand as one, supporting one another, loving the least of these, and serving Jesus as we serve our fellow human beings.

MICHELLE

My first date with Linda was on September 25, 1972. Providentially it was also the birth date of our oldest daughter, whom we wouldn't meet until ten years later.

Linda just seemed to know how to care for the lost. Maybe her training as a special education teacher or being the third of seven children gave her insights most of us don't have. She asked the social worker, after reading Michelle's two-inch-thick file, about our options for taking care of this precious ten-year-old girl who had been abandoned at age three and then passed from foster home to foster home. The worker said adoption would be ideal, but kids her age are often left in the system to live out their adolescence as wards of the state, sometimes in lonely places where successful human development is measured simply by how many years one survives.

When Linda told the nice woman that we would like to adopt Michelle, the woman's jaw hit the table. Her astonishment was rivaled only by the speed at which she switched the contract for foster parenting with the petition to adopt. On second thought, she wondered aloud, "Shouldn't you meet Michelle before filing the petition, just in case you don't like her or it's not a good fit?"

Linda's answer will always be the high-water mark of her beauty, grace, eloquence and compassion, as she simply responded, "Oh, that won't be necessary. After reading this child's file we didn't think she really needed to be liked. What she really needs is to be loved." So without meeting us first, Michelle arrived as a bewildered little girl with a suitcase in hand to be welcomed in as a Roley. I said, "Hello, I'm your Dad," and showed her to her small room. As she filled the dresser with clothes and the closet with coats and shoes, we were glad to know she would not need that suitcase again.

So our oldest daughter Michelle came to the Roley family in 1983 just months before her eleventh birthday. I loved her immediately. Though our twenty-plus years together have had some ups and downs, it is clear that Jesus blessed me with the amazing privilege of being her dad. God has used her to teach me so much about the ministries of mercy. She blessed Linda and me with our first grandchild, a beautiful boy named Benjamin. The circumstances in her life made it impossible for her to raise him, so he has his own adoptive family to join her in caring for and loving him. Our family remains in contact with and supports his new family in the fullest way we can.

MATTHEW

Our firstborn son Matthew is a wonderful free-spirited twenty-five-year-old full of talent and personality. He is married to Kelly Edwards and they have a heart for people, especially little children. Matt worked part time at The Vanderbilt University and Hospital's daycare looking after a gang of three-year-olds. His songwriting keeps him busy entertaining at local Nashville clubs, while his contributions to our family continue to be generous and timely. He struggled as a five-year-old when we placed his older sister in line ahead of him. I regret the tensions placed on him, first to be the oldest and firstborn, and then suddenly to be the second child with a whole new set of rules to live by. I couldn't be more proud of Matt, who continues to bring the message of mercy to those he meets and a consistent respect for God's creation and the environment so many of us neglect.

EMILY

Our second-born daughter Emily was four years old when Michelle came into the family and she, like her brother, was forced to deal with an older sister when she was very comfortable in her role as Dad's little princess. Emily showed her heart early in life when at age ten she gave all of her birthday presents to poor children in the neighborhood. She matured beautifully and in the fall of 2002 married a wonderful young man named Brad Smith. It is especially satisfying to watch them with the family and community using their wealth of talents as writers, singer-songwriters, musicians, photographers and friends to reach out to those less fortunate. Emily suffered through a life-threatening disease several years ago, and much of her empathy for hurting people comes from living with the memory of constant pain.

In the summer of 1986 Linda and I were saddened by the loss of a pregnancy that had been a complicated ordeal. As a result Linda went from not bearing the lost child to realizing she would not be able to conceive again, and her lifestyle would have to slow down, never to be the same. As she recovered over the next several months, we made some important decisions. We moved from Nashville to Franklin, Tennessee, to plant a new church, taking up residence in a house on Meadowgreen Drive. Linda regained her health, and we took a much-needed trip to England, Wales and Scotland, where I recorded a final album titled *Brother to Brother.* She traveled throughout Britain, hitchhiking, walking and riding trains, and staying in bed-and-breakfasts armed with her backpack and camera.

JEFFREY

Coming home that fall we prayed for a chance to adopt a fourth child and felt that a special-needs baby was again what we were destined for. As we sensed God's leading, it was about a year later that he provided an infant boy and our prayers were answered. Jeffrey Scott Roley was born December 17, 1987, and was introduced as our second son on the afternoon of the nineteenth, thirty-six hours later.

Jeff, or "Sage" as I call him, is of mixed race, and no one is certain what combinations are in that makeup. We immediately felt his presence in our family as he introduced us to the world of triracial people, which is a beautiful demonstration of the gospel, celebrating heritages and ethnicity, because of our oneness in Jesus. We began to enjoy those wonderful combinations of color and race that make up what the real American dream is about.

THE COURTHOUSE

Jeff is a bright and intuitive child who helped me understand the Christian doctrine of justification in a way only his insightful mind could share. The Roley men have a habit of overdriving the downtown traffic circle in Franklin Square, which is at the heart of our city's business district. It's a traditional traffic circle comprised of two lanes with a Confederate soldier's statue and monument in the center surrounded by banks, stores, the city hall and the high-profile, historic county courthouse on the southwest corner. The way we do the driving is to get to the inside lane as quickly as possible and then just hug the circle speeding our way around fast enough to press passengers, discarded McDonald's french-fry containers, book bags and any other loose objects up against the passenger-side windows.

One day when Jeff was about five years old we were driving around the square, and he surprised me by yelling out, "That's where I was born! That's where I was born!" He repeated himself until I slowed down the car and was able to understand what in the world he was talking about. You need to know he was born in Nashville, not in Franklin, at the General Hospital, twenty miles from where we were.

As the car stopped he was pointing at the county courthouse repeating, "Daddy, that is where I was born." It became clear what he meant. We have a precious videotape of our family gathering together three years earlier at the county courthouse on the occasion of Jeff's adoption. A judge made it official when he brought his gavel down and declared "Jeff to be now forever a Roley."

The judge reminded us that adopted children cannot be disinherited under Tennessee state law. Natural-born children can be left without a dime, but kids who are adopted are forever equally entitled to their parents' estate. Wow, the biblical truth of Jeff's observation knocked me out. Yes, Jeff was in a way born right there. His young remembrance of our videotape triggered the right idea. He was declared a Roley, taken from the status of being an orphan and brought into the status of being an adopted son. He was in a sense born again. He was forensically declared a Roley, a member forever of our family.

We, all of us, like Jeff, are declared God's children, adopted sons and daughters forever to be with him in the family of God. Jesus did the legal deal as he died on the cross, and God declared his righteousness to be ours. We receive Christ's righteousness because of his substitutionary sacrifice, and we appropriate that reality by faith. He takes the death we owe because of our sin and gives us back abundant eternal life. His grace and mercy belong to us because of his justifying act.

After Jeff's adoption we spent time growing accustomed to and falling in love with our new baby boy. It was fun just enjoying the racial diversity he brought to our family. Comments at grocery stores and from acquaintances and distant family members who did not understand only confirmed our decision to adopt a multiracial child as the right thing to do.

SAMUEL

About four years later we felt the time had come to adopt again. With Jeff growing up eight years younger than his sister Emily, it seemed appropriate to add a little one behind him. As it turned out, the Lord had the perfect choice for us. Samuel Isaiah Roley arrived on the scene, and our world was expanded again with our fifth and final child.

Sam was two years old when we met him while he was a foster child of the Coleys, a family that stands out in our community as true disciples who care about empowering the disinherited. They have fostered and adopted so many children that I think of them more as an orphanage than a traditional household.

Like our family, they don't see their decisions to take in children as some heroic exercise designed to make God like them. Instead they seem more like a group of beggars throwing the corner of their warm blanket over the shoulders of a cold stranger, welcoming that poor person into their huddle of care and love.

They had been fostering Sam for several months. He was returned to foster care because of a disrupted adoption. We met him in the fall of 1991, and as we would with any African American child looking for a home, attempted to find an African American family desiring to adopt. When, after several months of prayer and searching, he remained available for adoption, we were thrilled to petition the state to officially make him a Roley.

That request was granted, and Samuel Isaiah Roley became our third son and the baby of the family. He is wonderful and so gifted with lots of artistic and athletic talent. His joyful personality percolates constantly. As he got older he had an ability to cheer us up through humor. For instance, he called Michael Jordan, "Momma Jo Bo," he defined his brother Jeff as "Yo my brother from another mother," and when he was hungry his chow call to Mom was "I need mo sum fin to eat."

Recently at a wedding I was observing all my children now grown up and gathered together. I noticed each of them expressing his or her individuality. I am so proud of them all and confident that the three special-needs adoptions of our precious mixed-race boy, our African American son and our beautiful eldest daughter have built strength and courage into each of us. Obeying the law of love costs us all a great price, and the picture in my mind of my children playing together, teasing, hugging, listening, laughing, crying and challenging each other is proof that God's love can conquer all of life's struggles.

For young couples, singles, more developed families (looking to fill in gaps around children), elderly couples with time on their hands, really any family situation today, adoption and foster care opportunities are a fantastic way to help children and people who are in deep trouble.

Again, in my opinion, because of the continuing racialization in the southern region of the United States, interracial Christian marriages and adoptions are a clear demonstration of the gospel and how God's desire for us to come together across cultures, ethnicity and economic barriers.

Many families have encouraged our family over the years. As I mentioned earlier, Dan and Terry Coley have led the way. David and Nicole Mullen with their children Jasmine and Max, or "Hashbrowns" as we call him, are a family who consistently open their home to strangers and needy people. This isn't always safe, but it is what God calls us to do.

Nicole is a Dove Award-winning recording artist whose song "Redeemer" was honored as the 2001 Song of the Year by the Gospel Music Association. David is a leader who has worked diligently in minority leadership development, always surrounding himself with young African American and Hispanic men and helping them find scholarships and employment. He and Nicole work to teach young minority artists the importance of faith in Christ and a life of sacrifice in serving Jesus.

My longtime friends Howard and Betty Tryon have lived out the gospel through their interracial marriage, and Howard's current work with Tony Evans's ministries in Dallas, Texas, will be a blessing for both "Praying for You," the Tryons' prayer ministry, and Tony Evans's great intentional work of racial reconciliation.

The Lord is opening areas previously closed to the gospel through wonderful opportunities for North Americans to adopt extremely needy children. International adoptions are now more accessible for American Christians. In our community in Franklin, groups of families are connected through international adoptions. Mike and Cady Wilson, Geoffe and Jan Moore, Hugh and Lisa Harris, the Knoxes, Florians, Coleys and Commers are among a growing group in our church who have welcomed children into their families from other countries. Steven Curtis and Mary Beth Chapman have adopted two beautiful girls from China. Steven Curtis Chapman used his profile in the Christian music community to start a foundation to offer financial assistance to families embarking on the expensive process of international adoptions.[1]

Back on the domestic front, a ministry designed to help ease the urgent need for foster and adoptive care in Davidson County and Nashville was called One Child, One Church. The program has unfortunately ended, but how it worked was the Tennessee Department of Human Services, with some 400 children on its rolls in need of foster and adoptive care, would be connected to the over 600 churches in Davidson County which would each take responsibility for one child.

If every church took just one needy kid we could eliminate, or at least greatly reduce, the need for foster and adoptive care programs in Middle Tennessee. As the idea was introduced it was interesting to see the poorer, primarily minority, churches accept the children and agree to follow through with the program. The wealthier, primarily dominant culture churches were less accepting of the idea. It seems shameful that the churches with all the financial resources rejected this innovative idea and the churches with less material strength to give were rooting for the program, knowing it was helping mostly minority children in need. The baby Jesus was not white. The baby king who adopted us all would be on a waiting list for a family if he were born today in middle Tennessee.

The Bible holds out a parable for us to interact with which speaks of the kingdom of God as a garden. There is wheat, and there are tares that choke the wheat. It seems to me that God's people, the wheat, are by the natural process of growth sustained by God and end their days flowering in the fullness of the Lord's redemption.

Maybe until that time some of us slow-movers see ourselves more as wildflowers instead of maturing wheat. Conversion to the "word and deed" call of the gospel through the ministry of mercy and a commitment to biblical justice isn't always an immediate experience for the average believer. We don't teach much about social justice from our pulpits, and it rarely makes Sunday school curriculums, so it is an education and communication problem.

As the Scriptures capture our minds and hearts with a vision for the harvest of souls, we are irresistibly drawn to the neighborhoods of need. We respond because of the deep love Jesus has so freely given to us and the overflow of his mercy and grace—which demands action from us to those with visible problems living all around us.

Just as fully mature wheat flowers and drops its seed to reproduce, the care for the poor that falls from Christ's followers is a picture of that maturity in the life of the believer. This represents our conversion to mercy. Not to be merciful to the needy and loving to the poor shows how far from true Christianity we have strayed. The orchards are indeed full of fruit but seem empty of workers.

What keeps us away from the harvest are any number of bad ideas and conflicts of interest. Some think individuals must accomplish these tasks of benevolence; some say church and government have the responsibility to clean up society's mess. These tensions keep people frozen and unable to move. God's love is the compelling reason for mercy, and it alone thaws the deep freeze of bad ideas about the gospel.

For Linda and me, the thawing began through realizing that Jesus was using his body, the church, to correct the false teaching we had embraced. Through scriptural truth we sensed a clear calling by the Spirit which strengthened our faith in Jesus, and, so armed with his Word, we moved into a new neighborhood.

We also joined a church for the first time. We chose First Presbyterian Church in Nashville in part because we sensed many in the congregation felt a calling to work among the poor. These people became the foundation for the future ministries developed in nearby Franklin's poorer communities. We could easily find the disinherited simply by asking what part of town they lived in.

It is well known that every community has an area or neighborhood that is bypassed because of the dangers present there. Drugs, alcohol abuse, guns, crime—all the negative side of life is a day-to-day reality in these places. We know where these places are because we avoid them at all costs. When Scripture reminds us of Jesus' command to take the gospel from Jerusalem to Judea, Samaria and the ends of the earth, it is the Samarias of our lives that represent the undesirable parts. We are called to care for the needy in word and deed in the most difficult communities across the world.

6   Franklin Community Ministries

I WAS ALONE WHEN I DROVE THROUGH THE OLD NEIGHBORHOOD known as Hard Bargain for the first time in 1986. Not far from my church or the center of town, the small community was visually sobering and the kind of place that is more often read about than seen. It can be described in words, but the full identity can be grasped only by the senses.

Hard Bargain is an exclusively African American neighborhood in Franklin, Tennessee, eighteen miles south of Nashville. It sits on a small bluff just outside the historic downtown district, dissecting the line once established by Union breastworks that were heavily assaulted in one of the bloodiest battles of the Civil War. In that wild and hastily planned charge, Confederates attacked the Union's well-manned defensive lines through thickets of Osage and a hail of gunfire from strategically placed artillery and countless repeating rifles.

Not much remains of the battlefield where the Southern hopes for the western theater disappeared along with over 9,000 Union and Confederate soldiers. The intensity and result of that five-hour battle seems absent from life in Hard Bargain, although the stifling apathy that hangs around may have started then. During that massive late-afternoon attack nearly 140 years ago, this section of the large battle-field was relatively quiet, ironically making this part of town ignored both in war and peace.

The name Hard Bargain was first used by a buyer who endured a difficult haggling session when trying to purchase the first parcel of property on the hill. As time went on it became well suited to the overall conditions that came and stayed in Hard Bargain. Coinciden-tally this area of middle Tennessee was home to the U.S. navigator hero Matthew Fontaine Maury, whose elementary school namesake in Alexandria, Virginia, was where I first discovered social work.

After the area was purchased and named, the community became home for many of the black tradesman of Franklin. Carpenters, blacksmiths, stonecutters, crafters, leather workers, and their fami-lies settled here to build their houses and a future. As they created a community they gave the neighborhood its beginning and history, and they brought life and culture to this gentle, unknown Tennessee hill. Today, Hard Bargain is bordered by a state highway, a large ware-house, a graveyard, and a formerly segregated elementary school, boundaries that reflect both physical and cultural definitions. These telling landmarks all speak to the community about its past and fu-ture as they surround it with contradictory reminders of both hope-lessness and promise.

The houses that faced the narrow road and greeted me when I en-tered the neighborhood from the highway were worn-out shanties no bigger than an average garage. The randomly placed structures had been built and maintained with whatever makeshift materials could be found, and most of the paint-deprived, smoke-colored wood was cracked and rotting. The small dark doors and broken-out windows both exposed the shacks' crookedness and revealed their near-com-

plete surrender to the conditions that seemed to make them entrap-
ments as well as homes.

Instead of the expected property lines found between suburban
houses, these unkempt shanties were separated by mud, weeds and
scattered piles of harvested scrap wood. Without proper founda-
tions and sitting almost directly on the ground, there was no need
for anything more than a cinder block, a small stack of bricks or a
railroad tie to be used for front steps. Some of the leaning, weathered
shacks were just one bad storm away from collapse, and I had already learned that a few of them had twice as many people living in
them as they should. If their condition were the criteria for resi-
dency, even a single person would be too much. That area was
known as Polk Town.

Across from the shanties on dirt-covered Eleventh Avenue were
the old cottages that made up most of the Hard Bargain neighborhood. The small houses were desperate for paint and attention. I im-
pulsively looked at each as if I were seeing one individual tragedy after another, all of them together forming a colorless tapestry of
despair. I actually counted the dilapidated homes as I drove through
the six square blocks that comprised the neighborhood—either a
sub-conscious effort to calculate the scale of suffering or a heartfelt
attempt to know the end of it. More than one hundred homes, all of
them losing their unaided fight with decay, were pressed close to the
road and to each other, narrowing the gaps that might allow one to
see a clear way out and reinforcing the image of a trap.

The properties almost all had at least one rusty collection of junk
piled up in the yard, orphaned metal heaps of bicycle parts, grills,
displaced pieces of equipment and furniture. I passed more than one
partially completed section of homemade fence doing nothing more
than providing a resting place for the junk.

As I leaned over the passenger side looking out both windows, I wondered if the refusal to throw things away came from a desire to keep anything that might be fixed and used toward a better condition. When I looked at the piles I saw no possibilities, only desperation and futility.

The discarded appliances visible in every direction made a few of the collections of stuff large enough to fill the yard. Some worthless washers and dryers had been thrown into the mounds of metal salvage. Others had been left on front porches, where the items on top of them declared them to be either a makeshift table or the beginning of another pile. Many of the rusted collectibles rested under humble clothing swinging from frayed clothesline strung across the small yards and tied to anything that would hold them. A few refrigerators sat along the side of the road, their ages revealed through corrosion and outdated shades of goldenrod and brown.

Contrasts with the suburban settings that I had lived in all my life were obvious, but I had to look closely to identify some of the specific details that were missing from the overall picture. Gutters, exterior lights, shutters and other common components of most American homes were missing from the worn cottages. They were sturdier than the shanties that lined the entry road, but still looked more likely to meet a wrecking ball than a remodeling contractor. The aged roofs were full of patched repairs and their sagging ridges formed a low, uneven skyline.

Certain houses had unmatched roofing shingles covering their exterior walls instead of normal siding. The plumes of smoke that rose slowly from Hard Bargain's chimneys were not pleasant reminders of the comforts of home, but painful indicators that houses whose windows and doors were covered with pieces of plywood or plastic sheeting were occupied by real families.

I wonder how many of my white friends have ever seen homes like these? They were only a block or two from one of the most-traveled roads in Franklin, lined with million-dollar mansions, but I'm sure very few, if any, of my friends had ever taken this pothole-filled "road less traveled." Here and in the shanties, many of the residents relied only on a stove or fireplace for heat and cooking, so they depended on the woodpiles kept close to the house. Some corners and outside walls were blackened from fire, unrepaired like the damage from other accidents that marked homes on every street.

I was riding over a layer of trash that blanketed the community and seemed like it moved around but never left. There were no sidewalks in Hard Bargain so there were no street drains. Garbage collected on the narrow ribbon of dirt and grass that separated the houses and the street. The faded paper, bottles, and cans spread between the homes and in the yards. In some spots the rain and traffic had worked together to press the flattened litter into the ground. This week's newspapers and last week's leaves mingled together wherever the wind took them.

The streets of the neighborhood were old one-lane roads pockmarked with craters and stains, not much wider than the horse paths that lay underneath them. Vandalized abandoned cars were taking up space where there was none to spare, and collections of old tires were piled up or leaning in various places throughout the community. A small fleet of shopping carts from a nearby grocery store was scattered everywhere, parked in front of houses and in the empty spaces between the cars and near the street corners. The poor condition of the roads and the lack of any speed limit or other signs, combined with realities like those uncollected refrigerators, highlighted the degree to which official recognition or interest was still missing from the community.

Seeing the starkness from my truck, I realized how much the homes that my family had always lived in had been enhanced by nature. The appearance of the neighborhood was worsened in that there were not enough flowers and trees. Those that were there were barely surviving in odd places that were isolated, not integrated. Even a bright sun failed to bestow needed cheer since it served mostly to illuminate all of the neighborhood's afflictions.

The lack of any natural beauty and the signs of a piecemeal existence made the place look like a puzzle that was not quite put together correctly. Unlike most suburban neighborhoods, the homes were not joined with each other and their surroundings through planned community symmetry; the cottages were side by side with other mismatched homes and trailers, a design born in poverty and not in the mind of an architect.

After my numbness caused by the painful living conditions began to subside, I took more notice of the people who were hanging around in pairs and threesomes. If there was not some life and noise outside you might determine that the neighborhood gave up its inhabitants decades ago. Adults and children were gathered around front steps, sitting on parked cars, leaning on fences, occupying anything that offered a place to sit and hang out. There was talking and yelling, music, some young men passing a bottle, an old man watching the passing cars, some doing nothing at all. The porches were small but big enough for two chairs and the tired people who sat in them. I was recognized by a few of the locals well enough to have my wave returned, but most just looked with suspicion at the stranger driving through. It was not hard to understand why they wondered what I was doing in their neighborhood; I was not sure what I was doing there either.

The armed struggle once fought there did not decide the battle of identity that still goes on, a conflict between the people who live in Hard Bargain and the surroundings that daily affect decisions about their worth and future. The neighborhood unwillingly inherited an identity issue from the town around it. Franklin is a community whose past and present have not yet come to terms with each other or with the future that wants to force a merger on both of them. Such a confluence would require an ocean of reconciliation. For now, the lingering spirit of the Confederacy is confronted with the hopes of the new South, of a new Franklin. A painful history mingles with modern expectations, white ideologies cross paths with black dreams, and priceless antebellum mansions share space with Hard Bargain shanties.

Franklin's quaint streets and traditions are enough to offer an appealing persona to the world outside, but they are unable to satisfy the legitimate but sometimes restless interest in something more than what is here. We live in a world where the fulfillment of a dream could produce your brother's nightmare, and such contradictions generate their own angry clouds and divisive tornadoes, damaging human hearts and raising the cost of reconciliation. Hard Bargain is evidence of that. The hope that still survives is pressured to leave the area and go someplace where there is more room and interest. For now, one individual's wealth accentuates another's lack, somebody's mansion creates a cold, domineering shadow for someone else's shack. Despite the antagonism and the distance between them, they spin together in the same world and cannot escape one another. They define each other. Hard Bargain may wish to blame Franklin for its poverty and well-endowed Franklin may turn its back on Hard Bargain, but denying it's there doesn't make it go away.

The incarnation put God into flesh. He came and dwelt among us. It remains the single-most remarkable story ever told and the foundational truth to all good stories. Jesus relocated as he left heaven for earth. He knows us. When we see the needy it is only because we've been given his eyes of discernment. He shows us our need and points us to each other. When historic Franklin is mentioned in conversation it is often easy to forget the African American citizens who built most of her antebellum homes. The rich and poor are inseparable.

Like an underachieving sibling or an understudy to the real thing, the community of Hard Bargain exists under the oppressive shadows of both nearby affluence and human despair. The vapors of prosperity and not its substance are all you will find there, since the loan officers, builders, investors, and even the pizza deliveryman have no reason or desire to come. The shadows cast by other ways of life are felt, but the reality behind them remains firmly in other places. Here only the harshness of age, poverty, and neglect is seen up close.

As I drove out of the neighborhood, past the shanties, I decided that the people of the neighborhood must spend so much time outside because it was easier for them to feel human under the sky than under a leaking roof, and because it just feels good to the instincts to get out from under something. As I made the left-hand turn that would take me out of Hard Bargain and back where I came from, I was trying to get out from under something too. It was easy to leave the physical poverty behind, but I feared that an equally destructive notion would be coming with me, the self-centered love that would tempt me to forget what I just saw and tend quietly to my own affairs.

I was going home to Meadowgreen Drive on the other side of Franklin, where I would sleep soundly in the suburbs on the upside of the economic hill. I would not have to stay in Hard Bargain, where nothing is shiny and new and where the only dependable delivery is a fresh wave of discouragement pounding the neighborhood daily. I had gone in to look at the neighborhood in order to continue a social justice ministry that would serve the poor in our immediate community; I drove out having seen all that I had expected to see and then some. Most of the things that we would hope to find in a neighborhood with some longevity were simply not there, and all the things we fight against were a part of its life.

ORIGIN OF THE NAME

My daughter Emily, my wife, Linda, our church's youth worker, Paige Overton, and I left the Motor City on a pretty November morning. We smiled as we clutched cocoa, tea and coffees, trying to warm up and come to grips with what we had just heard, touched, seen, smelled and in every way been challenged with.

Detroit, Michigan, was the site of the third annual Christian Community Development Association conference. Several hundred community developers from around the country had gathered there to attend seminars and hear plenary speakers challenge us to work among the poor for the sake of the gospel. It was John Perkins's philosophy of reconciliation, relocation and redistribution preached and lived out. We had seen the videos and read the books, but witnessing it in action was what took us over the top.

Here truly was a strategy of word and deed ministry flowing from the truth of the gospel and calling all good-hearted believers to follow. We were willing sheep responding to the words of our Good Shepherd, excited to see in Franklin, Tennessee, what we had seen in Detroit—Christian societies and ministries reaching out to meet the needs of people who lived in neighborhoods like Hard Bargain, Baptist Neck, Rolling Meadows, Shortcourt, Reddick, Natchez, Cadet and Liberty Pike. We had witnessed the real deal and wanted God to build the same authentic work among our friends at home. We were praying about what to call our infant ministry and how to organize what we knew would be an outreach founded on relationships that God was beginning to develop.

The van was lurching up and down and side to side on the rough interstate highway leading us south out of Michigan. Paige was praying for us and the trip home, and as she closed her prayer she asked the three of us, "Why not call our work Franklin Community Ministries?" It was perfect. It gave our location in Franklin, it spoke to our corporate philosophy and unifying mission and also let people know right up front that we would be a faith-based organization. It would not simply be social work, but rather a covenant community of care.

Reconciliation, relocation and redistribution would be central to the philosophy of FCM. John Perkins, along with his disciples Dolphus Weary and Timothy Keys, would help us design this outreach effort to fit perfectly with our Franklin neighborhood's needs. And so, Franklin Community Ministries was adopted by consensus as Christ Community Church's ministry for biblical justice that fall in 1990. We had been challenged and called, and our hearts were inflamed with the truths of biblical social justice. We could not wait to share it with our southern Presbyterian coworkers at Christ Community Church, as well as our growing number of friends within the African American community in Franklin. We were sure there would be an overwhelmingly positive response to the work God was calling us to.

The obvious fault with that thinking was the misguided belief that we alone had the answer and must force everyone to do what *we* thought was right. Instead of seeing the opportunity in front of us to share our vision with others and to do Christian community development together, it seemed more and more that we would slide down the slippery slope of the top-down heresy. That is the wrongful teaching that we who have the resources must go and save the ones who have nothing. It reflects the myth of white supremacy as it attempts to ease the guilt of the oppressive dominant culture. It boils down to the almost subconscious belief that if you are born privileged somehow you are better, you obviously deserve it, you've earned it even in the face of the truth that none of us picked our heritage, our ethnicity, parents, geographical and economic circumstances. This sense of deserving or being better, though subtle, is pervasive in the culture. It moves into racial arenas because of the high minority percentages among the neediest of our people. Minorities are the majority of the poor. If you engage the poor it means that you engage minority people groups.

Part of the Detroit awakening was getting us in touch with a celebration of our diversity as people. The gospel was driving our reflections on the past, the reality of the present and the hope for conditions where our hearts would find a breakthrough into the mixed future described by Jesus' vision of life "on earth as it is in heaven." We were starting to see racism for what it was, a surrendering of intellectual wisdom to welcome notions and folklore at its worst! What was beginning to happen in our minds and hearts was surrender, not to the failure of love, but rather to the One who created ethnicity.

THE NEIGHBORHOODS

One year earlier I was the newly hired youth pastor at Christ Community Church. My office was in the historic Corn House on Third Avenue South in downtown Franklin, a building owned by the church.

It was less than a five-minute drive from the sanctuary to any one of the several socially disadvantaged neighborhoods hidden among the beautiful mansions of downtown Franklin. The past six months I had been frustrated by the growing need for a full-time mercy ministry at the church. My duties as the youth pastor were consuming, but the clear calling on my life and understanding of our call as

Christians to mercy ministry had ignited a desire to be among poor people in our rich city. Williamson County is among the wealthiest communities in the United States. We lived among an elite upper-middle class as stable and rooted as any in the world. In the midst of it all was a growing percentage of people struggling to stay just above the national level of poverty.

"Scott, there is a lady here to see you," said Barbara Pollard, the church secretary. I emerged to greet a troubled young mother. Her name was Caroline Hayes. We sat and talked, and from the conversation it was clear her son was struggling with life decisions and bad choices producing bad consequences. Christ Community Church was almost all white. Caroline Hayes was an African American. I agreed to see her teenage son Anwar and his cousin Robert.

Later that day I drove out to meet them at their backyard basketball goal in the Cadet neighborhood of Franklin. It was a little disheartening because they were playing the local street basketball game of 36, a simple-enough contest where scoring points totaling 36, or 18 baskets worth 2 points each, gave an individual the victory. You can play 36 with many players because of the solo nature of the game. Team play and strong defense (my self-proclaimed specialties) were not required.

I sat in my car and asked God for the grace needed to get somewhere with Anwar and Robert. I needed to play a decent game of 36 and prayed the Lord would give me the right questions to ask to show I cared about their souls. My fear was they would see me as someone trying to relieve white guilt or to flex dominate culture muscles. God answered my prayer. I played well enough to initiate a great conversation and to begin a several-years-long relationship with them both.

Youth ministry and community development fit like a hand in a glove. The vision from Scripture continually preaches families as essential to Christian community. Young people are critical to the church. For the next five years of my ministry, the incubator for Christian community development would be the Christ Community Church youth group. Over the years through its various directors, assistants, interns, staff members and a host of volunteers from different Williamson country churches, relationships were formed and programs built to meet needs revealed by those friendships.

Our community of caregivers was responding to the biblical teaching from our pastors and others whose tapes and books were influencing the strategies and implementation of our programs. They taught us basic Bible instruction about how care for the poor starts with the fundamentals. God created the earth and all that is in it. It was all good, very good. When Adam and Eve fell, the perfect relationship with God was lost.

The Fall, therefore, included all of creation, spiritually, psychologically, materially, and socially. It was Jesus who rescued that fallenness. He came to earth as God and man. He relocated among fallen creatures and through his cross and resurrection redeemed for God all that was gone. Jesus restores with new life the spiritual, psychological, material and social wasteland, and when he completes the task, he declares it the new heavens and the new earth.

We get a small glimpse of that when we put a roof on a house in Hard Bargain or bring dinner to a rich family whose parent is wasting away with cancer. It seems to show up when we reflect on the goodness of God in the midst of our misplaced anger, fear, frustration, disappointment, other sins and need for repentance. Love can be expressed by the simple act of collecting newspapers and magazines so that our neighbors can stay warm at night. Each of these exercises in faith done by the believer is an entrance into the realm of God's kingdom where he is reclaiming his people and property. For us, Christian community was defined by the relationships we shared as we worked in God's kingdom. The reasons God gave us through Scripture joined us to him in the mystery of his ways and joined us to each other in the depth of his mercy.

Understanding the scriptural basis for care for the poor requires a lifetime of Bible study and living out the truths found there. If you did a simple study on the words poor, poverty and justice you would be amazed at the number of verses concerned with social justice and issues of oppression.

The Bible teaches that we should talk to God about our lives and especially about situations and relationships that seem to be unfair or unjust. Because God has committed himself to redeeming the new heavens and the new earth, our prayers to him about the poor and how to relate to them and their issues are essential to accomplishing his will. Prayer for every kind of need is appropriate. In fact, prayer is so fundamental to the success of God's plan for the poor that it is always more important than programs. I mean by prayer the sincere, heartfelt, Spirit-directed, Bible-regulated exchange between Creator and creation. God speaks and we listen, we respond and God speaks again. He speaks by his Word and Spirit and we trust him by the same. We listen to him together in community. We are therefore first and foremost a community of faith listening to Jesus who instructs us to love the poor. It is a great adventure to hear from God and enjoy relationship with him. It is out of this rich heritage that the joy of serving the poor blossoms and finds meaning.

Jesus' presence is unending. Our prayer life is to be that constant. First Thessalonians 5:17 calls us to pray without ceasing. God's river of unceasing mercy spills out with true love for those in deep need. Biblical principles for the ministry of mercy are so plentiful that a case can be made for the entire Bible being God's declaration of his commitment to the poor. The Bible is a manual for Christian community and how to care for those in need.

Jesus is the ultimate community member, the perfect developer. He comes to serve. He shows the way God desires for us to act in laying his life down for his people. Jesus dies on the cross serving us and calls us to do the same. We obey by laying our lives down for each other.

Of course, Jesus' substitutionary death on our behalf saving us from the death and hell we deserve is from him and him alone. Only the perfect Son of God could save a dying people; it is not our call to save anyone. Jesus is the Savior; we are his servants. Often we get that turned around and we feel the pressure to be the savior of the poor.

Nothing kills momentum in a ministry of mercy like confusing the motive of *serving* with the motive of *saving*. So many disappointed Christians walk away from opportunities to care for the poor because people would not respond, get better or act the way they were expected to. Our expectations of what people should be like are destined to be frustrated, and often we feel like failures or that God is not at work. The results simply do not live up to what we hope for. Ephesians 6:7 and Matthew 20:28 remind us that to be servants is what our calling is about.

For example, early on in the work of community renewal Paige Overton ran a girls' Bible study and I ran the boys'. We called the study "The Deal" using Carl Ellis's wonderful covenant study of Scripture to teach the gospel. A year into our time together, my young men were beginning to get into trouble with the law, some of them being arrested and put in the county jail. Paige's girls were experimenting sexually, and several of them became pregnant. We didn't abandon them but sought ways to help.

A strong jail ministry emerged as we visited the boys behind bars to pray with them and offer help as they were released. An outreach called Safe Harbor was started to care for pregnant teens. We were somewhat frustrated; it seemed all of our efforts were failing. If we had started the ministry to save these young people and keep them out of harm's way, then it looked fruitless. However, simply serving these fantastic kids was our privilege and joy. We are still in relationship with many of them and their children, some of whom are enrolled in our school New Hope Academy and in the ongoing Eagles tutoring program.

After Carolyn Hayes's son Anwar and I met and spent time together, another mother and grandmother in the Cadet Lane area sought help from our youth group. Mrs. Odee was looking for a youth pastor to be a part of her church's new members drive and revitalization efforts. I was asked to preach at the Lynn Creek Tabernacle and was very excited about the opportunity. Preaching in black churches is inspiring and spiritually invigorating. More importantly, I was able to draw close to Mrs. Odee and her three grandsons. The boys became our good friends and regular members at the Bible study.

Paige and I drove my '78 Toyota Corolla, painted bright green by the junior high football team I helped coach that fall, into an underprivileged neighborhood near the church. Paige was a vibrant twenty-five-year-old white woman with a heart to serve Jesus. She was convinced our church should reach out to the poor beyond traditional storehouse ministry. She had the energy needed to be the hands, heart and feet on the streets and in the homes establishing community development. We pulled up to the back door of Mrs. Odee's home in the Cadet Lane/Liberty Pike community. As a typical white youth pastor and an unlikely looking community developer, I'm sure we scared off many potential friends in the neighborhoods.

We knocked on Mrs. Odee's door and as she opened it we all smiled.

I did some awkward introductions and then we sat in her back room with cold drinks and talked about life. Mrs. Odee was not shy about personal struggles, and the more we inquired the more she shared what type of help would be useful. Paige and I listened and thanked her for her kindness. We explained that we would be calling on her regularly and that we were interested in her grandsons and granddaughters enrolling in youth Bible studies that would soon be starting up.

As we left we had no idea that the mode of our ministry would not change much for the next ten years. It would be meeting people, discovering through the relationships their prevailing needs, and then working on ways to meet those needs through the resources of combined churches, fellowships and Christian societies—connecting people across race, denomination and economic divides. As we drove back to the church we committed ourselves to work day by day on the relationships God was providing and not worry about programs, funding, advertising, recruiting, etc. We would pray and ask Jesus to show us what he was doing. We then vowed to follow him and do those things by faith.

So many opportunities to minister came from those relationships. When Paige, who had been an inner-city school teacher in Nashville as well as the administrator of an overseas mission organization, came on board with our junior high ministry it was clear her calling was to mercy ministry and care for the poor. Without a job description or a budget to work with, we decided to start the community development ministry in Franklin.

My experience had been that through a variety of gatekeepers like Caroline Hayes and Mrs. Odee in each economically deprived neighborhood we could find acceptance and a welcome into the community. My encouragement to Paige was that all she had to do each day was get up, knock on doors, introduce herself and ask the residents what needs they had. To this day that's still all any of us really do. We make friends with our neighbors and through those relationships are exposed to needs. Meeting those needs with deeds of mercy is what Christian community is about.

THE GOAL NOBODY COULD TEAR DOWN

From the first time I laid eyes on our new church's facility purchased from the First Baptist Church in early 1985 I was attracted to the idea of a basketball goal. Our neighbors across Fourth Avenue South at First United Methodist Church had a rugged backboard on a telephone pole in the middle of the parking lot, which lured a host of ball players when cars were not filling the parking spaces. It seemed our layout between Fourth and Third Avenues South was the perfect cover for a court that could be easily lit for night games as well as protected daily from parked cars by church property wrapped around it like a coat. The first goal went up and we waited. It took several days for the basket to be discovered, but once the neighbors knew it was there they turned out in waves.

At first we had a cheap backboard acting like bait to see if kids would really come to play. They tore it down in about a week. The next one lasted almost a month, ending its days with the rim bent straight down. These young people could get up high and hang on and dunk and crash the boards and rip down metal, twine and poles like they were knocking down snowmen. The next several basketball goals were increasingly sturdier. When we added the lights on the side of the sanctuary, play lasted late into the night. Often on weekends it was well past midnight by the time we stopped the games.

When the fifth basket was knocked down in our third year as a ministry I went to one of our deacons asking if he could put up a goal nobody could bend. He said it was possible, and he delivered. The goal George Kennedy placed on that playground stood for ten years until the property was sold, and the post itself had to be cut with a torch to bring it down.

Many relationships were forged in the intensity of three-on-three tournaments or just pickup games of 36. Who knows how many families the staff and volunteers of FCM were able to meet because of that simple basketball goal? It drew us together in the way only physical exercise can, sweating, bleeding, getting angry, breaking stuff, the real life battle between the haves and the have-nots. In the shadow of the church's steeple and across the deteriorating parking lot from the Williamson County Courthouse these games were staged and played.

Boys and girls without fathers and mothers, dropout teenagers who needed direction, older mid-twenties alcoholics, and unemployed ex-athletes, along with middle class and upper-middle class youth workers and members of a community church were all trying to find common ground; it seemed for now to be on the court under a goal nobody could tear down. In the midst of the wealth of historic antebellum Franklin, sons of former slaves and sons of former slave owners played ball. Ten years later there would be other common courts and goals as Christian societies flowered to meet needs all around our town. Many of those most important and high-priority needs were recognized in the midst of the heat of churchyard basketball games.

HOOP NIGHT JAM

Paige and I were serving as Bible study teachers for the neighborhood junior high students who were coming to the meetings to play basketball, have some cold drinks and just talk about Jesus' deep love. We soon realized that to be more effective with the predominately African American young people we would need male African American role models.

It was our desire to develop minority leadership all along, but the potential loss of the students because of our inability to relate just hurried up the process. Providentially the Lord's leader for our ministry was right on time.

As it turned out Jesus' man of the hour was a young African American rap artist from Baltimore, Maryland, named Christopher Wesley Williamson. We did not realize when he was hired as the intern for FCM that he was as gifted a preacher and orator as any of us had seen or heard for a long time. He relocated to Nashville after being educated at Liberty University and Seminary where he won every award they gave for preaching. His rap group had recently abandoned a major-label recording contract, and all three members pursued full-time pastoral ministry.

Pastor Chris, as he has come to be known, was the catalyst of leadership needed to bridge the racial distance among the young Bible students. And as a team member he was invaluable at connecting resourceful wealthy church members with economically disadvantaged families. The Lord used Chris to plant the seed of relationships that eventually flowered into Strong Tower Bible Church. Its intentional cross-racial distinctive continues to be the high-water-mark for racial reconciliation in Franklin.

Early in his ministry Chris Williamson sponsored a three-on-three basketball tournament called "Hoop Night Jam." The winning team took a road trip with Chris to see Michael Jordan and the Bulls play in Chicago. Over four hundred participated in the all-night event, with lots of action: a big fight at 3 a.m., threats of guns, knives and hostility. All the tension you would expect among young people from economically disadvantaged neighborhoods, frustrated with struggles most of us above the poverty line never experience. It's the same thing everyday—families in trouble, few decent paying jobs, legal injustices, schools that can't help much, a county jail clogged with friends and relatives, a lack of great heath care, roofs that leak or are falling in, drug and alcohol addictions, etc. The despair that comes from living in the dominant culture of the South when you are a minority is a way of life, where the majority never has to learn your culture, but by necessity you must learn theirs. This breeds a quiet resentment that surfaces when people of all races and class structures sit and talk about their problems.

The goal nobody could tear down was something of a metaphor for Jesus, the Man at the center with open arms to welcome us. He relocated to our neighborhood, our churchyard and courthouse parking lot. He stood at the net caring for each of us. He spoke his love to us and challenged us to love as he did. We spilled out into the communities we came from with his mercy and grace. Jesus was the servant leader and we followed him. Could it be the Lord was directing the changing of a city by simply helping us enjoy the wonder of a game of 36?

It made sense to me that God used the fabric of everyday culture to reveal his plan uniting his people. The community church's downtown location and dedication to welcoming young people from different cultures resulted from a desire not to steal members from other churches. It was important to make clear to the students they would be embraced if they had no church home, but if they were connected to local congregations we hoped to support those churches as well. Even with such a demonstration of the gospel there were members of Christ Community Church complaining of damage done to the facility, which is what happens when children play hard; sometimes things get broken. Maybe we need to remember that facilities are there to facilitate ministry. While we focus on the people of our congregations, the gospel also calls us to concentrate on the strangers and lost souls outside the church's doors.

7   **Empty Hands Fellowship**

RETURNING FROM THE DETROIT CONVENTION WITH OUR EYES opened to the depth of the racialization in our families, churches, cities, states and nation forged a commitment among us to look for relationships in need of reconciling. It was obvious to all that we begin with the churches in the socially and economically disadvantaged neighborhoods of Franklin. The pastors and lay leaders laboring there would be a great group to start with.

Unfortunately we didn't do enough follow-through from that conviction. We made attempts on various occasions to enter the lives of the African American pastors in Franklin. The men who made up the target group were easy enough to find. They met monthly under the banner of the Franklin Ministerial Alliance.

The FMA was the epicenter of successful Christian leadership in the African American community but the FMA was not necessarily seeking an integrated relationship with its Anglo counterparts. In hindsight, what should have happened first was my simply knocking on the door of Franklin's First Missionary Baptist Church and inviting its pastor, Denny Denson, to join me for lunch or a time of prayer.

Instead I retreated into my own bias, prejudice and racialized cowardice, which froze me on the first step of the staircase leading to the historic First Church's front door. Each time I determined in my mind to go meet Denny and discuss our mutual needs and how we might together create strategies to meet them I choked on my fears of anticipated failure and lost confidence.

Jesus was the only one who could change my heart of pride. Even my young friend and associate, Paige Overton, was struggling in attempts to bridge the racial gulf in Franklin. Several occasions produced nothing but frustration and discouragement as she found a cold reception among leaders who were suspicious of a church that would send young women instead of the male pastors to begin a church-to-church relationship. Valid criticism emerged from the simple fact that we did not know each other, leaving plenty of room for distrust. Their legitimate questions of how long we would stay and why we cared were somehow hard to answer. We would need time to demonstrate our sincerity and calling. The Franklin Ministerial Alliance seemed closed to us and remained somewhat suspicious of our activity. We contributed to the division by not communicating well and going about our business as if we didn't need them.

That kind of insensitivity was eventually brought to light, and we changed our strategy. Our optimism was dampened by a reality that seemed ironic. Franklin Community Ministries' name was born in the shadow of the disappearing Renaissance Center as our rented Ford van headed down I-75 South out of Detroit that fall day. The Renaissance Center was built in celebration of the economic renewal of southern Michigan decades after the country's industrial revolution brought thousands of southern African Americans north as laborers to satisfy the nation's hunger for automobiles. Fifty short years after emancipation, strong minority arms and shoulders would be lifting and holding up for all to see the objects of status that fed majority culture need and greed. The division between the haves and the have-nots would widen, and it was a sign of what we felt in Franklin. Only the God who brought a renaissance to our hearts as individuals could now bring us into true community.

Franklin Community Ministries paled next to the mighty renaissance going on in the big cities. I wondered if, in God's plan, FCM could be Franklin's Renaissance Center. Could each of our hearts be renewed and regenerated and if so, where would all that tender mercy, unconditional love and immeasurable grace spill? Maybe renewal in the middle of our quaint southern town was exactly what God desired and demanded of us. We were little, weak and ignorant, but he was big, strong and full of wisdom. Remembering back, it seems right that on a bright, clear, cold autumn afternoon in the shade of Motown's finest structure a new vision was born: a new name given, a new Franklin, Tennessee, to be encouraged and admired, and a new South to give our hearts to for the rest of our lives.

ROCK OF AGES

Several years later, Dr. William Lane, or Bill as he insisted his boys always call him, was enjoying his Egg McMuffin and orange juice on a crisp autumn morning just as he had each Wednesday during the fall of 1997. He was taking his seat at his favorite table and joining the other faithful brothers who met together to eat breakfast and just talk about the struggles and successes each were experiencing on their journeys of reconciling across the divides of race, economic status and Christian denominations.

New friends and first-time visitors were welcomed with an interrogation about who they were. Then there followed a detailed explanation of the purpose of the group. On this particular morning, after a new brother had shared his heart, someone from the group mentioned the insight he received recently after listening to, and studying the lyrics of the famous Christian hymn "Rock of Ages." The gospel leaked from each stanza of the hymn, especially the one that reminded the listener "nothing in my hands I bring, simply to the cross I cling." It was at that moment it happened.

"It is the essence of the gospel," Bill slowly said in his clear, unmistakable voice, a voice full of tenderness and truth, a voice that resonated with boldness and humility. His character shined through his voice with the same intensity whether he was defending his doctoral thesis before a board of Harvard University scholars or asking directions to the walking path near Mammoth Cave National Park in Kentucky. His voice simply made you want to trust him. He quickly followed the statement with an explanation that we come to God without any agenda. We don't come demanding anything, expecting anything, or deserving anything. Our only hope for God meeting us at all is found in the comfort of the knowledge that he has already moved toward us. He has reconciled us through his cross by relocating to earth from heaven and empowering his people by his Spirit to live by faith. As Bill finished he insisted that that was indeed a good description of those sitting down together enjoying breakfast. "We are the men with empty hands; we are the men of the empty hands fellowship!"

That classic hymn which gave the name to our ragged little group continues, "Naked come to Thee for dress, helpless look to Thee for grace, foul I to the fountain fly, wash me Savior or I die." The Rock of Ages, Jesus, serves us well in defining the hearts and mission of the Empty Hands Fellowship. We cross racial, cultural and denominational differences in our desire to build lasting Christian friendships. It is about our brotherhood in Jesus. We know each other's birthdays, children's names, wives' names, big-time dreams, sizes of living room

The Empty Hands Fellowship, November 1997. Back row (left to right): Ben Johnson, Mike Smith, Bob Smith, Scott Roley, Hewitt Sawyers, Steve Green, Walter Amos. Front row: Chris Williamson, Denny Denson, Tom Moucha, Michael Card.

television sets, favorite sports teams, music groups, etc. I even know what kind of toothpaste Denny Denson uses, because we shared shaving kits in West Africa while traveling together when his luggage was lost. The EHF is not about big agendas, big deals or big ego trips. We only want to be close to each other because Jesus wants that. It just seems right!

Leading up to all of this wonderful fellowship were ten years of struggle and frustration trying to reach out to one another and continually failing. Over that period, several breakthroughs eventually led to our coming together. In terms of the broader community, Pastor Chris Williamson, like Paige and me, was not extremely successful in breaking through to the original Franklin Ministerial Alliance. He was young, an outsider and an intern at a large, white church. It would take several years for him to win the hearts and trust of the brothers. In the end he has done so as the Lord used a series of providential events to bring us all closer.

At the same time during these years of pursuing racial reconciliation among the underserved families in Franklin, another white pastor was making headway with a different group of reconcilers. Tom Moucha had extended fellowship to several black brothers in the Franklin Ministerial Alliance. He was being received and welcomed. It was a profound racial breakthrough.

Tom eventually helped connect the future Empty Hands Fellowship with Franklin's traditional black church, and his reconciling efforts were critical to the success of our community. Today Tom, and his former associate pastor Dr. Ben Johnson, continue to lead the way in the reconciliation movement as they demonstrate shared leadership in their congregation at Franklin Fellowship Church. Dr. Johnson, or Dr. Ben as we call him, is a true patriarch in the movement for racial reconciliation. Internationally known within Christendom, his twenty years as an African American professor at the Moody Bible Institute and his many other years as a pastor, author, lecturer, concert performer and missionary have connected him with thousands of Christian brothers and sisters who are active in the ministry of mercy and care for the poor. Dr. Ben was close to Dr. Lane before Bill's death, and the two of them fathered the Empty Hands Fellowship through many hard times.

Another important movement was happening among Chris Williamson, myself and Hewitt Sawyers, pastor of the West Harpeth Primitive Baptist Church on the south side of Franklin. Early in my ministry I heard of Hewitt Sawyers and had met casually with this remarkable African American pastor and civic leader. As the only native Franklinite among our group, he was familiar with all the past hor-

rors of discrimination and oppression. And he saw the progress being
made by many civic groups trying to bridge the racial gaps left in Williamson County after two-hundred-plus years of slavery, Jim Crow,
civil rights fallout and postmodern denial of any problems.

We met at Choices Restaurant on the corner of Fourth Avenue and
Main Street in Franklin. As we shared a meal, we both realized God
was calling us to a commitment and that regular meetings for prayer
and fellowship were essential to our developing a relationship. The
purpose of spending time together would be simple fellowship, demonstrating our hearts for reconciliation.

We began meeting at the West Harpeth Primitive Baptist Church
on Tuesday mornings for an hour of prayer, and then Pastor Chris
would join with us on Wednesday mornings for breakfast at the Mc-
Donald's on Highway 96 West. Our three churches, Christ Community, West Harpeth Primitive Baptist and Strong Tower Bible Church,
also met together and began to worship quarterly on Sunday eve-
nings with blended music, prayer, testimony, sacraments and preaching. We called the worship gatherings harmony services and rotated
them quarterly among the three congregations on Sunday nights.

The response to these meetings was overwhelming as each time
the church sanctuaries overflowed. Our largest service was held at
Franklin High School because its auditorium would seat over 800,
and we knew at least that many from our congregations would attend. Chris Williamson, Hewitt Sawyers, Mike Smith, a newly added
member of our small group working as an associate pastor at Christ
Community Church, and I had decided that after several years of
meeting we needed to expand, and because of Hewitt's prominence
in the Franklin Ministerial Alliance, he felt he could extend an overture to bring us all together.

It worked, but not as we had planned. Tom Moucha, Ben Johnson and Denny Denson had been meeting for prayer on Thursdays much like we had been meeting on Tuesdays. Denny was the pastor of First Missionary Baptist Church, which he describes as "the gateway to the ghetto." His strategic congregation sits at the entrance to Baptist Neck, in the Natchez Community. He was the gatekeeper and the one man able to unite all of us in one solid movement of reconciliation.

Hewitt Sawyers brought the idea of solidarity to Denny, who was reticent, not because he didn't desire reconciliation but because he doubted the motives of a large white church that for years had sent people to do tutoring, housing renewal projects, youth camps and other programs but in all that time had not once stopped to ask for his advice, permission or help. It was a deep hurt and one that I took personally. I had hidden myself cowardly behind Paige Overton (our FCM Director) and Chris Williamson (our intern, now the Pastor of Strong Tower Bible Church). I had never walked up to Denny and extended my hand in brotherhood and friendship expressing my sorrow for the years of separation our races and denominations had endured. I never told him how embarrassed I was that after ten years in Franklin I had not once stopped to enjoy fellowship with him, his wife, Lelah, and the members of First Missionary Baptist Church.

Hewitt Sawyers brought the report of Denny Denson's hesitation to join forces and explained why. I immediately got up and went to where Denny, Tom Moucha, and Ben Johnson were praying. For me, looking back, it was one of the most defining moments of my life. I headed in the front door of First Missionary Baptist Church, up the same stairs where I'd frozen before. About halfway down the aisle I encountered a strong, handsome African American man with his arms open, a smile on his face, his eyes lit with tears and the joy of the Lord exploding around him. Choked with emotion, I blurted out who I was and that I was so sorry for my stupidity, failure, cowardice and the shameful ignoring of his presence, position, leadership and potential friendship. I was a fool and Denny realized it.

Instead of beating me up with "I told you so's," he embraced me and wept with me. He heard my apologies for slavery, for inconsiderate actions throughout history, my own racist attitudes, and my fear and failure at not trusting Christ to draw us together. He responded with his own repentance for judging me by others' wrong doings and for his years of racist attitudes as a member of the Black Panthers and other militant groups. We held each other long and hard, and any time I need to remember how my black brother feels toward me, all I have to do is close my eyes and go back to that embrace. It was the day Jesus held me through the arms of a black brother named Denny and assured me that as sinners we were going to navigate the difficult waters of racial reconciliation, and whatever I would face in life was covered by the healing power of that forgiving embrace.

It was not the first time all seven of us were together, nor the last. Unknowingly we had all been at the final Harmony service months earlier held in the auditorium of Franklin High School. Tom Moucha, Mike Smith, Hewitt Sawyers, Chris Williamson, Denny Denson, Ben Johnson and I enjoyed sweet fellowship that day and vowed to continue the meetings. From then on we did them together.

So on Wednesdays we met at 8 a.m. in the playland at the West 96 McDonald's. We would then meet for prayer on Thursdays from noon until one o'clock at FMBC, and afterward break for lunch at KFC or Mrs. Winner's before heading to afternoon ministry duties.

The breakfasts gave us time to relate and fellowship together. We also heard each of the brothers' testimonies about coming to Jesus and their calling to the reconciliation movement. In the following weeks Michael Card and Bill Lane joined our meetings and by November 1997 helped establish a steady flow of brothers coming to both gatherings. We were self-named and proclaimed, through the wisdom of our own Bill Lane, the Empty Hands Fellowship.

With Dr. Lane, Mike Card and Mike Smith came the Franklin House Study Center, where serious Bible students could go and study under the likes of these men. The study library was absolutely one of a kind, and students came from all over to use it. After Bill's death it remained a central hangout for the men of the Empty Hands Fellowship, whose devotion to Dr. Lane was overwhelming and who received from Bill love and leadership beyond words.

Importantly, many other societies in our city focused on racial reconciliation, and the Christian community development flowered in Franklin in part because of those works.

The Tapestry ministry was a cross-racial, -denominational and -cultural ministry to women in Williamson County. Members joined in weekly ministry meetings in each other's homes throughout the year. They concentrated intentionally on placing women in groups with sisters who stretched their comfort zones. The year-long program culminated in a luncheon where all the Tapestry women's groups and an invited public met at a local church. The lunch featured Barbara Skinner, a national speaker whose ministry was dedicated to caring for the poor through racial reconciliation, creative connectional reneighboring, and empowerment of disinherited people.

Paige Overton and a group of prayer partners were instrumental in this ministry's great success. Laverne Holland, assistant to the headmaster and office manager at New Hope Academy, as well as the president of the Mt. Hope Community Association, helped tremendously in seeing reconciliation move forward.

Also, the Eagles program initiated through FCM by Paige and Cady Wilson has for the past ten years been a premier program, helping tutor and mentor elementary school age children and upper-school teenagers. Cady Wilson, the current coordinator of FCM, and her staff at the Franklin Community Center continue to reflect and demonstrate racial reconciliation and empowerment for the poor. The downtown Storehouse Ministry, which handles walk-up clientele, has been managed and directed by several key African American women who are developers and important members of the community.

Events and occasions for celebrating our diversity as Christians are always something we look forward to. Six members of the EHF had the opportunity to travel to West Africa, which was a profound experience. More than anything else, we simply love being together. Any excuse to hang out and live our lives is enough for us to drop everything and do it. We love to eat together and go to various functions, watch our children's events and family affairs.

I've been to Denny Denson's family reunion; he's been to our family's big Thanksgiving dinner. We've spoken at and attended each other's churches, traveled and done speaking engagements, sometimes riding in Michael Card's tour bus for days. It's not unusual for us to share cookouts, barbecues, Tennessee Titans games, movie outings where we watch a film like *Remember the Titans* or *The Hurricane* and then spend hours talking about what we've just seen.

We have discussion groups about books we've read or topics like politics, education and world events. We meet, rain or shine, each Wednesday and Thursday, even if our meeting day falls on Christmas or New Year's Day, and we've been doing this faithfully since the fall of 1997.

The everyday sort of time together has blossomed into year-round events sponsored by the Empty Hands Fellowship. For instance, we have a meeting each January to celebrate Dr. Martin Luther King Jr.'s birthday. A march, rally or worship service on or near the national holiday helps us remember the past and look to the future to see how

far we still have to go. We've done yearly spring revivals that rotate
from church to church much like the old Harmony services.

We support the National Day of Prayer organization, and our habit
is to gather on the square in downtown Franklin, praying together
with the public for our civic leaders, churches, families, schools and
any other needs from our community. Prayer is the absolute foundation to any and all Christian work. It is fundamental to all of life. The
Holy Spirit of God changes hearts. There is nothing we can do to
make someone receptive to care for the poor or racial reconciliation.
We not only pray on Thursdays but also often schedule all-night
prayer vigils at various locations where we literally spend the night
in prayer. The sweet fellowship with the Lord and with each other as
a result of these prayer events reminds us to see our life with Jesus as
a continual relationship of prayer.

THE GATHERING

The ultimate Empty Hands Fellowship event has come to be known
as The Gathering. It happens in late September on a Sunday evening.
We block off the square in downtown Franklin and usually have music, videos, praying, preaching and testimonies about what God is
doing in our city and county in the area of reconciliation. We attempt
to cross over race, denomination and economic hurdles to worship
God, and the response has been fantastic. Several thousand people
from all backgrounds—Anglos, African Americans, Mexican Americans, Latino, Hispanic, Asian and Native Americans—gather with
one voice to call for the love of God and love of neighbor.

The Gathering is simply the spilling out onto the streets of Franklin what is flowering from the hearts of the people, a movement from
the darkness of segregation and subtle southern apartheid to a new
South, where we are intentionally working together to relieve the suf-

fering of injustice. It reflects a deep calling to reconcile our racial problems living together in unity, helping each other in tangible ways, and reinvesting in people who feel they've been left out. In 2000, several thousand people gathered to hear the inspirational songs of Steve Green and the soulful offerings of former Doobie Brother Michael McDonald and saxophone great Kirk Whalum. Among Whalum's many accomplishments is the sax solo for "I Will Always Love You" performed by Whitney Houston in *The Bodyguard*. Michael Card also provided music that night, singing the Empty Hands Fellowship's theme song, "The Basin and the Towel." We have used Michael's music at many events, especially during footwashing services and revivals.

A gathering in the summer of 2003 featured well-known Native American recording artist Bill Miller sharing his testimony of growing up on a reservation in Wisconsin, the Lord's work of mercy in his life and how the Empty Hands Fellowship embraced him. When EHF president Lynn Owens preached the gospel that night, it was translated into Spanish by EHF secretary treasurer David Green. Also speaking was Pastor Jose Duran, who, along with members of his church, My Father's House, joined us that evening. David's brother Steve Green, the internationally known Christian singer, published a collection of devotions written by members of the Empty Hands Fellowship. The book, *Morning Light* (Harvest House, 1998), shows the deep relationship the Greens have with the fellowship.

A final note about our programs: In 2002 we had a go-cart race to raise money for societies working for racial reconciliation. The ERACE foundation (Eliminating Racism and Creating Equality), sponsored the event and, with racing legend Daryl Waltrip and other sponsors, the Memorial Day race was a huge success. More and more events dedicated to reconciliation efforts are bringing out large numbers of people ready to move on, to repent truly for their failures to love each other, and to commit themselves to supporting one another in every area of life.

INTENTIONAL RECONCILIATION

My pastor and discipler of twenty-five years, Scotty Smith, and I recently sat with a wonderful African American candidate applying for the headmaster position at New Hope Academy. This private elementary school was founded with the mission to provide a quality classical education to economically disadvantaged children alongside children from middle- and upper-income families. Again, it was an example of two unlikely white guys interviewing an African American brother who we would submit to as the authority over the school in the same way we submit to Denny's authority as the former president of Empty Hands Fellowship.

African American leader Chris Williamson, pastoring the multiracial congregation at Strong Tower Bible Church, preached the opening services for our larger white church's new facility just two days before the attack on the World Trade Center and Pentagon on September 11, 2001. In fact, Denny joined Chris, praying in the inaugural services for our church and community. Scotty and I, along with the several thousand members of the congregation, submitted to these gifted, called preachers of the Word of God. These examples of intentional submission help ask the question, when was the last time any of us submitted to a leader from a minority culture? Unfortunately all too often our answer is never.

Reconciling racial differences is difficult and must be intentional. One struggle is that dominant culture leaders rarely are called to submit to minority leadership. Michael Card and I were sipping hot coffee out of foam cups at the McDonald's near Hillsboro Pike and Old

Highway 96 on the west side of Franklin. We were sitting at the particular table where we used to hang out with Bill Lane and other founding members of the Empty Hands Fellowship. We were waiting for our friend and brother Denny Denson. He was an unusual buddy for the likes of us. His southside Chicago, Illinois, upbringing, military tours in Vietnam and membership in the early '70s militant organization The Black Panthers seemed as different from my northern Virginian country-club heritage as the sun is from the moon. We had become best of friends. The other original members of the fellowship met with us later for breakfast at a larger, new location. We were forced to leave the McDonald's playland to accommodate the growing number of brothers who desired to submit and share their lives with other men across racial, denominational and economic divides.

We were experiencing the gospel's powerful call to celebrate our diversity, watching racist attitudes disappear. Mike, Denny and I met often outside the appointed fellowship times, enjoying our friendship. These relationships began as intentional colaborers in God's kingdom, but quickly matured into a deep brotherhood.

Denny and I had just returned from a speaking engagement in Atlanta, Georgia, where we shared our story with young men and women working as youth pastors in various churches concerned with the issues of racial reconciliation, reneighboring and empowerment of the poor. Often we are asked to share what's going on in Franklin with a variety of audiences.

Racial reconciliation is simply sharing together the overflow of God's reconciling mercy. It is the essence of the gospel, which reminds all of God's creation that as sinners we deserve the eternal separation from him reserved for those who refuse him. His mercy to us, and the grace that saves us through faith in Jesus, flow out to those God calls us to love.

Shamefully, before my intentional move toward the African American brothers in the Empty Hands Fellowship, it was only African American sports team members or fellow musicians that I befriended. Even then it was not with the mindset that these men's families would go vacationing with mine, or that perhaps my sons and daughters would fall in love with and marry their daughters and sons. It had been my misunderstanding through a prejudiced southern upbringing that taught me to ignore people whose skin color was darker than mine. Not looking in the eyes of people who were different from me points out my pure ignorance and unnecessary fear.

Through groups such as the Empty Hands Fellowship, the ERACE Foundation, the Tapestry ministry, and other ministries and organizations, I've seen an entire community begin to embrace one another in new ways. The story of this change in my thinking and also in the minds of so many others was the journey of facing personal and corporate racism.

BENIN

Although I had been there ten years earlier, as the jet doors opened the anticipation of a new adventure and the mystery of Africa took over. The smell of the Dark Continent was unmistakable. The power of the Beninian drums and the rhythms of the dancers who met the plane mixed with the suffocating heat to create excitement.

As we were led down the airplane's gangway onto the tarmac it all felt wild but good. My compatriots sensed they were home. We were five lost souls finding paradise, like starving men dropped into a West African kitchen searching for food to satisfy our deepest human hunger, the hunger for origins. The hunger to understand why the three black brothers of our party, along with millions of others, had their forefathers stolen from this place. What would they find?

Contonou, Benin, was the city chosen for the reconciliation conference. President Matthew Karakou had called for the return of the diaspora of Africans from Europe, the Caribbean Rim and the Americas. The purpose was to apologize for the West Africans' role in the Atlantic slave trade from the fifteenth through the nineteenth centuries. It was Africans apologizing to Africans. These were the apologies of the middlemen, the wholesalers. Where were the apologies of the beneficiaries, the European traders and American colonies?

Denny Denson was my roommate for the week, and, unfortunately, the airline lost his luggage so we had to share my clothes, deodorant, cologne and toothbrush. The Third World is a tough place, even with the smallest comforts of home, and to Denny's credit he didn't let it bother him at all. In fact, many people commented on how fine he was dressed and how great his aftershave smelled.

Moments of repentance, remembrance and forgiveness highlighted the weeklong conference. We stood on the beach at Qui Dah thinking about Denny's, Hewitt Sawyer's and Chris Williamson's ancestors and what they went through as they were herded onto crowded slave ships after being forced through the "gate of no return." We wept together like children and held each other because the hurt was just too much to bear alone. The loss of history, heritage and family name has the obvious effect of dehumanizing an individual. However, better understanding what happened brought our fellowship closer as we agreed to reach out together, holding onto our adoption in Christ and our commitment to each other. We realized clearly that we were family.

So many people are like me in that it takes a unique event or an unusual occurrence to put us face to face with our racial bias. I was confronted first by the Dr. Martin Luther King Jr. "I Have a Dream" speech as a youngster in the early '60s. I realized through my formative years that I was fearful of dark-skinned people. Browns, blacks, and darker shades made me less likely to look the person in the eyes or to touch them. I felt better just ignoring people who, after my conversion to reconciliation, would become my closest brothers and sisters and even members of my family.

As a result of the adoption of my younger sons I have been given the gift of adopted blackness. Because of my sons, what I thought were the harsher skin tones are now by far the more appealing colors. Before my sons, I held an unexplained prejudice against cross-racial marriages. It was racism, pure and simple. After my sons came to me, I began to feel like I was in some ways now African by adoption. I think cross-racial marriages and ethnically blended families are beautiful and really do demonstrate the gospel to a world that needs to see love with skin on, in word and deed.

I am looking forward to years of enjoying the relationships Jesus has given me through my family, church and the Empty Hands Fellowship. Who would have thought that my desire to get involved with care for the poor through racial reconciliation, creative reneighboring and empowerment would come by way of the innocence of two wonderful sons—sons whose multicultural heritage showed me my foolishness and humbled me, who raised in me a boldness to celebrate my acceptance by Jesus into the world of racial diversity.

Denny and I are often invited to speak on racial reconciliation. We were at a breakfast meeting in Nashville and were introduced as members of the "Helping Hands Ministry." As we stood to begin our presentation, we stopped long enough to make sure everyone listening knew we were not from the "Helping Hands Ministry." In fact, we resisted saying we had anything at all to give that would be helpful.

Being helpful was a wonderful desire, but what we truly represented was the Empty Hands Fellowship. We come to Jesus' cross with no agenda, no big programs. In fact, any of the wonderful events that surrounded this ministry and have been helpful to people are only an overspill of the grace and mercy we've been given in the relationships we share across race, denomination and economic divides.

Christ has adopted the enemy. He has adopted us. His call to us in Scripture is to do the same, to adopt the enemy. Those we think we could never love become the ones God uses. He shows us our deep need and failure as well as the depths of his love for us. My perceived enemy has now become the way of salvation.

The racial tension in our southern culture, though kept beneath the surface, is so powerful that it is almost unbearable. We all stand together on a societal platform that is possibly the greatest expression and most successful experiment in the exercise of human freedom, the U.S. Constitution. The document, which protects our amazing freedom, ironically has no power to secure rights for those omitted by their ethnicity and a failure to fit the majority culture's definition of personhood. This glaring deficiency is not because of language. The words of protection are right there to read. The failure is in deeds.

The Bible is a book of books, all about words and deeds, and it forces us to ask of our government's books the same questions about holding us to standards. Our walk must reinforce our talk. Language and practice must play a concert together. The letter and application of Jesus' call to deny ourselves, take up the cross, and follow him is the only answer to our inconsistency. It is in facing the past, reckoning with it, and then looking at what is happening today that gives us the input needed to move forward. As pastor Tim Keller of New York's Redeemer Presbyterian Church reminds us, too much focus on the past narrows our insight. Too much existential focus leaves us shallow and without substance. Only in surrender to Jesus and accepting his calling is the path made clear. Through prayer, trusting his Spirit, we move forward in his will.

THE CROSS BURNING

Cross burnings are ugly, ancient, evil, hateful demonstrations of supposed racial superiority. Just the words bring to mind the painful past of white-robed cowardice and black innocent fear. But that was early-twentieth-century stuff, a thing of the past. *Those kinds* of things just don't happen today do they? Dateline: Franklin, Tennessee, May 2002.

One of my youngest son's best friends was a graduating sixth grader from New Hope Academy. He had a cross burned on the front lawn of his house in a working-class neighborhood while his single mother and two siblings watched the entire frightening scene from their bedroom windows. The police response was to first call it a child's prank and then to simply move on. Fortunately, because of eyewitnesses and pressure from the media, the story did break. The Christian community responded by supporting the young single mother and praying with her and her children and also for the one who committed the awful act. Anyone with a sense of history and an understanding of Franklin's culture would see that this incident was the worst of misguided humor and realize that all perpetrators involved needed to be prosecuted to the fullest. Simply put, this was terrorism.

If we sidestep these opportunities to truly communicate with our African American friends, to say we are outraged and sorry, we will never get closer to each other and the heart of mercy and the hope of sharing our lives in community will remain hidden. Wherever the heat of hatred is hottest we are called to move into it and bring the deep love and lasting peace of Christ. Each member of Christ's body is called to work with the other members under his sovereign headship and by his Spirit's power. We are not authorized to live self-centered, independent, careless lives. In the deepest parts of our hearts we know we need God and each other.

I remembered our family's experience with a cross burning and how it connected with the recent events in Franklin even though it happened thirty-five years earlier.

My dad was speaking my name softly but firmly. He was telling me to get up and follow him, in his cool, calm "it's an emergency, but don't panic in a crisis" voice. My brother and I obediently stumbled downstairs behind him, our eyes still sticky with sleep and minds clogged with interrupted dreams. It was too early to be up, even for a fishing trip, and as I passed our hallway clock it screamed 3 a.m. at me in the middle of dead silence.

The staircase led us down to the front door where we could see orange light flickering as if Dad were still burning a late-night log in the fireplace. The only problem was we didn't have a working fireplace in the house. The firelight was coming from the front yard. As we all turned our faces toward the living room bay window, the sight sent a chill down my spine and out my mouth in a gasp. There in our newly mowed grass was a five-foot-high cross burning like an uncapped oil well. It was lighting up the yard, house, street and neighborhood for all to see.

The shock, disbelief, fear and worry began to sink in as my father asked calmly, "Do you know who that is?" At the edge of the darkness and flames stood a very young man with a can of gas, smiling nervously. I immediately recognized him as a socially awkward fellow student from my ninth-grade class. This all happened in the spring of 1967 while my family was living in Bloomfield Hills, Michigan. That area of southern Michigan was one of the wealthiest suburbs of

Detroit as well as one of the richest cities in America. We lived only a ten-mile drive from Detroit's toughest ghetto, but we might as well have been on the other side of the planet.

Fast-forward thirty years. About fifteen of us from Empty Hands Fellowship stood next to each other, hand in hand, and prayed for the African American mother and her three precious children. We also prayed for the young white man who several nights earlier had burned the cross on the front yard of the woman's home. A white neighbor had called 911 while they were still observing the boy in the act of doing it. Many older African Americans in our group remarked that one positive in all of the confusion, fear, terror, anger and dumbfound shock was that the white neighbor had responded, when only a few years ago a white person would not have necessarily called the cops. The tendency then and now is to simply look the other way and feel badly but not badly enough to really get involved.

I don't think the young student back in 1967 knew what he really was saying by burning a cross on our family's lawn. We had just relocated from the southern culture of Virginia, and he thought the prank would be taken lightly as a joke and as something cool. My father had a loaded Winchester rifle that he intended to use that night. He knew exactly what the sign of a burning cross meant and found nothing clever about it at all.

The young cross-burning man in Franklin was reportedly involved with an anti-African American group who thought these kinds of acts were helpful in scaring single moms and young children out of the mostly white neighborhoods. Crosses are frightening—frightening enough without setting them on fire.

Our young single African American mother of three is staying put, and all of us are sharing the responsibility of standing against hate and the fear it brings. Maybe Jesus' cross is what we need to see today.

It burns with his consuming love, making him beautiful and believable. It gives value to all who gaze on its wonder and are warmed by its tenacious affection. Didn't the Romans scare their enslaved peoples with crosses, and didn't they burn Christians crucified after Jesus' death and resurrection? We all need to embrace the cross—not as a symbol of terror to try to scare people, but rather as the symbol we pick up as an act of love. After all, didn't Jesus say if you will be my disciple you will deny yourself, take up your cross and follow me?

By the way, the young man from Franklin who did the cross burning was sentenced by a circuit court judge familiar with the Empty Hands Fellowship to serve six months public service at the Mercy Children's Clinic, a pediatric clinic for low-income families. His probation was overseen by the EHF and he has become a good friend to all. He is a reconciled member of our community.

To me, the South is one of the last great places to live on earth. Civilization's most shining outpouring is called Franklin, Tennessee. The factors in our town that stand against consistent racial reconciliation are numerous. Franklin's Civil War battlefield, one of several spots claiming to be the bloodiest in U.S. military history, couches the new battlefield of racial reconciliation. The great short-story writer Flannery O'Connor described the South as "Christ haunted" versus "Christ centered" and her assessment seems true.[1] There is a religious Christian Jesus that peers over the shoulder of southern people. This is a haunting reminder that Jesus' true presence and desire for relationship with us gives us great hope for a *new* Franklin and a *new* South. As we surrender our fear of diversity and then collapse on the one who created all color, we see the dullness of a white-only world give way to the celebration of beautiful shades.

8   Relocating

I WAS STARTLED AWAKE BY GUNSHOTS, AN OCCASIONAL EXPERIENCE
in Hard Bargain, and then proceeded with my usual response: roll
over and go back to sleep. I rose several hours later to the news that
five African American neighbors were wounded by gunfire earlier
that Sunday morning while they partied late, the Saturday night cus-
tom at the local American Legion drinking club 150 paces from my
front door. The story of the shooting barely made the local papers
and there was no television coverage.

The unconcerned response came in sharp contrast to local reaction to an earlier similar event. The spring before my family moved
into Hard Bargain, a white man from outside the county had been
shot and killed by a young African American teenager who was a resident of the neighborhood. The teenager had fired a single round into
the bed of the victim's pickup truck attempting to intimidate the man
after the drug deal they had both agreed to went bad. The bullet ric-
ocheted, tragically killing the man. That incident, of course, made all
the papers and was shown repeatedly on television. Again, it happened at the corner of Glass Street and Eleventh Avenue, only three

houses from mine. People who live on Glass Street shouldn't throw stones or fire guns at white people, but it pretty much doesn't matter what they do to each other; it is a simple lesson to learn.

Stories like these happen every day in urban America; however, Franklin only sees violence like that every twenty years or so. We do, though, experience daily the sense of inequity between dominant culture white perceptions and minority culture views of reality. Mostly those are of African Americans in all class structures, along with a continually growing population of Mexican Americans, Latinos and Hispanics who do day labor and trade work, and a small but vital community of Native Americans. Lord have mercy.

This obvious need for mercy across all groups of people is sometimes hidden from view. True hope for mercy is also our real need. When the hope for mercy disappears, our vitality for life goes with it. Hope drives community. It can be covered up by endless messages that seem to say real community is impossible. The hidden heart of mercy and the lost path of hope all too often characterize day-to-day life in Hard Bargain. Hope returned as I remembered back six years.

FROM MEADOWGREEN TO HARD BARGAIN

Depending on your viewpoint, it could be either a simple two-mile drive or an incredibly wild journey; to me it was both. Two miles were all that separated my old neighborhood and my new one, but the real distance between them could not be measured in mere miles and could not be crossed in a car or my old Land Cruiser.

As I drove the last load of boxes downtown, I knew I was not a brave pioneer daring to venture out and single-handedly cross a cultural divide. I knew that it was not true that I was navigating some dangerous water on my own and should be proud of myself. This move was an opportunity given to me, and it was more than could

A house in the Hard Bargain neighborhood.

be carried with a human grip or by my bad hip and knees.

The many barriers of race, economics and culture that divided this town were beyond my full comprehension, let alone my ability to overcome them. Aren't those barriers really found in places that I can't reach anyway? I found the comfort and strength I needed in knowing that there was good news, that the hard part was already done. Somehow grace had crossed the many unseen valleys of separation that lurk in the human heart, something only God could do. The Redeemer had conquered those divisions that hinder relationships, and the way between all of us was now wide open. How could that be? How could that not be? Again, his mighty hand had accomplished the impossible task, and the way had been prepared. All I could do was just believe it to be so and drive the two miles.

My work as a pastor in town and the many meaningful relationships that had been built over time meant that the suburban development in my rearview mirror would not disappear from my life. It also meant that my new neighborhood was not seeing me for the first time.

The gospel reassured me that I wouldn't ever be alone here or anywhere else and that I should not waste my energy on worry. Instead, I needed to spend extra effort on asking myself the questions that the kingdom was asking of me right now. *Where is my heart at the moment? Am I holding the fullness of joy? Do I love the poor or the notion of loving the poor? Do I really want this to be my neighborhood? Could I live the rest of my life right here?* Not worrying meant that I would trust in him for this hour and this moment, knowing that I could no more envision next year than I could have predicted this day.

This neighborhood had found its way into the hearts of the caring and devoted people in Franklin long before I ever showed up in a moving truck. All of us were excited to see how God would bring the fruit of deeds from the richness of the word he had planted in our lives. Together, we felt called to yield to a grace so profound that, although you see what is happening moment by moment, you still feel like a bystander to your own life. We wanted to let the experiences that he was using to shape our hearts and faith be the basis for our ministry to the community of Hard Bargain and urban Franklin.

The personal and denominational creed of our fellowship was to glorify God and enjoy the journey, and Jesus was giving us a very real context for those words. In different ways, the Lord had brought each of us to believing that indifference to the poor was not just a political persuasion but also something akin to idolatry and murder. God's heart concerning the poor came more clearly into view as we studied the Scriptures and prayed together for help and guidance.

Many of us in the group also began to attend the conferences sponsored by the newly formed Christian Community Development Association (CCDA). These early conferences, like the one in Detroit, were reinforcing the idea of relocation as a foundation of ministry. I was shaken by the CCDA teaching that relocation began with Jesus Christ, who left the perfection of heaven and of home to live among the impoverished. I marveled at the thought of it, and Christ began to use my relationships to fan the idea into a flame.

I came to believe that his plans for my family and me included relocation. It was a personal calling—I sensed that I would fail in his service if I tried to balance his love for the poor with the habits of letting financial assistance or prayer be my *only* efforts to reach a needy neighborhood. Why was I letting some other ambassador represent my love through charitable deeds, when I was an ambassador myself? How critical to his ministry was the relocation of Christ? What I initially saw as a radical concept was now appearing to be an essential aspect of the ministry that we had been praying for. Christ purchased me with his own blood, not with a treasure chest of gems from the rich resources of heaven. Even if I could send millions of dollars into Hard Bargain, my compassion for the people would remain suspect if I refused to send myself. Distance is not a part of who he is. He chose no substitute when he came calling for me, and in following him I should realize that he has not changed his ways since then.

I'm still not sure if our desires were a realtor's nightmare or fantasy, but our minds were made up and without much fanfare we bought the home on Glass Street in November of 1997. Linda and I with our three older children made the decision to do it together. Michelle, Matthew and Emily had all finished high school and were out on their own, but our house would still be the place that they would call home during breaks from college and vacations. It would be here that the best family pictures would be hung, memories stored, and future spouses introduced. Linda and I needed to know that we were together on the move, and we were. Sam and Jeff, as school-age sons, were too young to cast votes, but they were excited by our enthusiasm and the hope of something new.

We had been looking for a home in this neighborhood for a long time, but the houses were usually passed down through the local families and were not on the radar screens of the rest of the world. If one did become vacant or available, the tractor company that owned the adjoining warehouse would usually purchase and destroy it before we could look at it. Their swift demolition practices probably came from an assumption that they were beautifying the place and that no one else would ever make an offer on a Hard Bargain home anyway. After many years, my friend Pete Volpitta finally told us about an old cottage that we might be able to buy from the owner before something happened to it.

When the time came, it was not difficult to pick this neighborhood. Each of the noteworthy community borders contained unlikely assurances for me to see. The huge graveyard that lies just across the street from the north side of Hard Bargain is segregated into two cemeteries known by two different names. Mount Hope cemetery is filled with prominent white people including Sarah Cannon (Grand Ole Opry star Minnie Pearl) and noted scholar Bill Lane, my friend and Bible teacher. Despite the location of his grave, there was no segregation in his life; Bill lived in close relationship and communion with his black brothers. In death his place was decided by the rules of color that govern the graveyard. The other cemetery holds the remains and the histories of most of the African Americans who lived their lives here. If you drove into or by the neighborhood from that direction, these cemeteries would be the most visible and stirring sight to greet you. When I occasionally walk through them or attend a service that is held there, I am struck by the bittersweet drama of living, the pain endured by far too many people, and the providential turns that life takes whether we are paying attention or not. If I ever need my own boundaries redefined or my reasons for moving to Hard Bargain reaffirmed, all I have to do is go there.

The black cemetery was built to honor permanently not only deceased residents but also Toussaint L'Ouverture, the Haitian slave and revolutionary leader who died seeking independence from Napoleon's France. When I saw the cemetery's historical marker dedicated to him for the first time, I was powerfully reminded of my own liberations, one of the greatest of them occurring on the streets of L'Ouverture's Haiti itself.

HAITI

Fourteen years earlier I was invited to take a trip to Haiti by an adventurous and mission-minded friend named Larry Warren. The country was in turmoil due to the power vacuum created when "Baby Doc" Duvalier left in a hurry with most of Haiti's limited supply of money. At the time, I was a vocational Christian singer-songwriter struggling to hold my own with recording contracts and a road schedule, and my friend wanted me to provide a music ministry to accompany his preaching. I quickly became excited about the idea, and before I knew it one of my music industry patrons wrote me a check for the airfare. Larry flew out a few days ahead of me, after leaving instructions on when and where to meet him. Even though Haiti was chaotic at that time, I wanted to seize the moment so I got ready to fly into Port-au-Prince in the middle of the tropical and political heat.

It was not very long before Haiti's national frenzy began to have an impact on my trip. I was the only non-Haitian on the flight out of Miami, and my plane was detained on the tarmac for over two hours as authorities worked to remove two suspect Creole-speaking passengers. When I finally arrived in the Haitian capital, I noticed that the large passenger plane behind mine on the runway was surrounded by camera crews, lights, and a large crowd. The humble airport terminal was also filled with people and sloppily dressed soldiers carrying automatic weapons, looking more in shock than in control. Tons of debris and wandering goats, chickens and pigs added to the chaos and confirmed that I had entered a different world.

In the noise and confusion, my excitement mixed with some fears as I looked for my contact. What was intended to be a simple arrival and pickup was beginning to look more like a rescue. It was nighttime, and I was mesmerized by the incredible feel of the place. The black faces of the swarming Haitians shimmered under the bright lights, whistles blew, small vehicles and bicycles darted everywhere, and the air was full of sounds and language that I had never heard. While I was trying to take in this incredible scene, I heard my name called. "Hey, Roley!" the voice yelled from the huge crowd in front of me. It was my friend Larry, fifty yards away and squeezed into the throng of Haitians. "Welcome to the third world!"

We soon learned that the floodlights and camera crews were American, and international television networks assembled there to catch the arrival of one of Haiti's exiled former leaders, returning in the aftermath of Duvalier's departure. The whole country was in an uproar, and everything was crazy. The atmosphere formed an ironic backdrop to our simple, spontaneous efforts to talk a little about Jesus with the people of Haiti. We felt like just another part of the whirlwind, but our visit seemed to bring some peace and smiles to the Haitians. Our little talks and short songs seemed a pitiful gift to bring for people living under such crushing conditions, but they were all we had. Small as it was, our offering of fellowship echoed with the promise of things they could not yet see but would someday be theirs. I can only hope that our words have remained with those precious people and their children as permanently as their faces have remained with me.

I was and still am astounded by Haiti. A personal liberation occurred for me as I changed my mind about many things after witnessing the pain. These souls walk through a life of poverty so extreme that their self-identity can be permanently branded by it. Their days are filled with the realization that there is no opportunity and no escape. They grow up within a boat ride of all that they desperately need but remain alone together with all the others who are chased by a dozen deaths until they can't run anymore. Since the days that Africans were first kidnapped and brought to this hemisphere and to Haiti, their lot in life has too often been dictated by someone or something else. After I saw the suffering up close, this reality left its brand on me too.

Many of my assumptions about the world simply died there, and their passing made room in me for new desires and convictions born out of that experience. It did something to me that visiting Watts and Harlem and living through the 1967 Detroit riots had not done. Feeling the drastic impact of slavery and poverty jolted me into understanding that America is too close to this Caribbean country (and not just geographically) to be completely free from the same afflictions. Although the degree is different, the lingering conditions in many areas of the United States still bring the same suffering for many of the same reasons. I saw a link between the suffering of the formerly enslaved Africans in Haiti and the hardships of the poor in America. When later merged with the idea of relocation and reconciliation, my time spent in Haiti became a spiritual compass, and the conviction sparked there is refreshed whenever I notice the little pieces of Haiti right here in my neighborhood. If I had not gone there, I never would have moved here.

Another confirmation of the move and an unlikely pleasure of Hard Bargain residence is the frequent blast of train whistles. They often roar through town, and you cannot live here and be unaware of them. My father is responsible for my love of trains and their sounds. From the time I was little, he built miniature railroads in our home, took me to look at trains in town, and even invited me along on a lengthy train ride to Atlanta, Georgia, just to feel the rumble. A mighty train whistle that blew during his funeral back in 1969 appeared an interruption to some of the grieving bystanders, but it was a promise of God's great comfort to me. Now I live close enough to train tracks to rest in that comfort twice a night. These sights and sounds were both assurances and a reminder that it is easier to assess and define something physical (like a neighborhood) than it is to examine honestly the boundaries of my own heart.

Maybe that is because the senses give me immediate answers to the casual questions, and it takes much more than that to see hidden things clearly. I did not think of myself as poor, but I sure was needy, and that would be true in this neighborhood or any other. This neighborhood can be as full of the gospel as any other, and that means that it is as good as any other place on earth to live. I was brought here to be blessed by a wealth that is a color other than green.

My new old house is smaller than our last one, and it did need a lot of work. All the paint was peeling, the floors were sagging, the plaster was crumbling, and the foundation was shot. There were small and large problems in every room, and we had to work on it for five months before we could move in. A longtime friend, Kenny Meeks, skilled in rehabbing old homes, served as our contractor. Many others helped out; we needed financial assistance and got it through our families, friends and the community of caring Christian brothers and sisters who also committed themselves to the principle of relocation. Imperfect or not, it was the substance of something hoped for and the perfect harvest to a long-term desire that had been planted and watered by Jesus alone. The house would meet the needs of our family and fulfill our God-given dreams. Linda was delighted to see that it had a real front porch, and I was happy that there was enough room for my guitars and fly rods.

After dark on the first night in the new house, I noticed an odd red glow coming from the bathroom. Some of the disasters and near-disasters that happened during the months of repair came to mind. *What the heck is that? Did we hook something up wrong? Is something about to explode back there?* I wandered back and looked around. The red light was coming into the bathroom window from the outside. *That's a relief. At least the explosion will be outside.* I slowly moved to the window and looked out. Everything was bathed in a light red glow. As I looked up I saw the source: a huge neon Texaco sign mounted on the roof of the gas station just behind us, far and away the most prominent thing around. It made the whole neighborhood look like we were about to have a close encounter with something from out of the sky. I didn't know which should worry me more, the ability of human beings to sleep while covered in red light or the possibility of a real explosion someday. I thought about organizing a community promotional day—Hard Bargain Tuesday or something like that—when all of the residents would buy some gas, and the station's owners would agree to turn off the sign for a night. I decided to think more about that in the daylight.

It is difficult to find anything in common between our home in Hard Bargain and the last one. Even the final contract settlement experience was different. Some of the normally commonplace paperwork was not easily completed because of missing or unrecorded information. No one was absolutely certain of the actual address of the property itself, and to this day we have more than one choice of numbers for our mailbox. When we bought our last home on Meadowgreen Drive, the deal was generally nice and neat. So was everything else—the lawns, the streets and the mailboxes. At the time it was just what we wanted to buy and right where we wanted to be.

I say generally nice and neat because there was one small thorn in the side of Meadowgreen Drive's suburban bliss. Looking back on it from where I am now, I think that maybe it was an early indicator that our future would be found somewhere else. After the deal was completed, our realtor threw out a casual reminder to purchase flood insurance, since the home was located in the 100-year flood plain. His words were prophetic, and we remembered them when we were slammed with floodwaters in 1993.

The night of the flood Linda called me home from a church leaders' meeting, and I found her in our bedroom up to her knees in water. We took a deep breath and together gathered our energy to move our furniture and other belongings. We stayed with it, but the water kept rising and soon covered more things than we could move, including our bed. It was too high to allow us to continue our salvage efforts. Linda broke down and cried as she grabbed her favorite Laura Ashley dress and headed for the safety of the second floor. We lost almost everything that had been in our library, bedroom, and garage. Ever since that night, thunder has been much more ominous, and the once-peaceful sound of rain brings anxiety and alarm to everyone on the street. Our dear friends the Southards took in our entire family while we spent six months rebuilding the first floor.

As bad as it was, the flooding was not what washed us out of the neighborhood. The suburban flight that took us to a place surrounded by gas stations, train tracks, police cars, graveyards and poverty was—unlike urban flight—a choice to go toward something and not away from it. I was free to do it or not do it, and I wake up every day thankful for that.

Legalism has always made me cringe, no matter where it came

from, and the law of Moses was no exception. I was always terrible at finding any motivation in laws, even the good ones. Because of my tendency to shrink from legal demands, I knew that I was being led by the gospel; I could never have done it if it had been initiated by duty. I needed to know that. Every person who mentored or influenced me on the subject of moving my ministry and family to a neighborhood like Hard Bargain had said the same thing: the gospel alone has the power to make it work. The gospel has been powerful to me for many reasons, but none more than the fact that it sets me free to move toward people. I can be sent out in his passionate purposes, liberated from the fears that cause me to misread even the goodness of the law. Unlike fear and legalism, the gospel gets me going by telling me about love, not just by instructing me in what to avoid.

For that reason, the move was more an acknowledgment than an achievement. Linda and I were moving our family and our stuff because Christ had already relocated our hearts to this place. Although we learned much during those months of preparing and repairing, one thing seemed to be an exceptionally clear message for us. We were seeing that it is a mistake to assume that his redemption stops its forward motion after we place our faith in Jesus Christ. We tend to become infatuated with the rest stops that dot the paths of our journey, but he presses on and pulls us along. When he does so, he teaches us that true rest and joy come only from his company. Living out that truth by abiding in him means that we have arrived, even if we are still moving. True wandering is not about finding your way; it is much more about staying focused on our God who is always on the move.

Real rest is found only in Jesus; he is the refuge. Our attempts to get it artificially by micromanaging a half-acre piece of the planet can cheat us out of the wonders that he has waiting on the horizon of our calling. His redemptive power and love keep moving in the souls of his children, always cleansing, teaching, loving, compelling. The inward joining of grace is tender but ambitious and will eventually affect our feet. When it does, he sets our hearts on a pilgrimage with a plan that he promises to see through as the author and finisher of our faith. He is not afraid of our future, and he will move and carry us until we are not afraid of tomorrow either. I don't remember that as well as I should. His redemption is so strikingly beautiful that I often settle for just the stained glass version, forgetting the faithful, scrappy persistence that wins victories in the dirt of my daily life. Beautiful and near, it moves me.

THUNDER AND RAIN

My big dream for Hard Bargain included building a relationship with William Murry, my new next-door neighbor. Despite being confined to a wheelchair after the amputation of one leg, his father-figure strength commands the respect of the neighborhood. He is the front-porch sentry of Glass Street, making the rounds in his motorized chair and making sure that nothing happens at either end of the street without his knowing about it. His will to see everything made better here is rivaled only by the youthful mischievousness that he has kept intact all these years. His wife, Katie, is a direct descendant of the first black landowner in Hard Bargain and a woman whose natural sweetness fills whatever house or porch she visits.

William and Katie have been married for more years than I have been alive, and they were grounded in faith before I got my first bike. Moving here brought me right next door to them and to a tremendous learning time in my life. *What will they think of my move and my theology and my ideas and my friends and my stuff? Who am I in light of what they have been to this neighborhood?* Upon my arrival on moving day, William's smile and wave said all I needed to know. His face was not twisted with worry over my impact on property values. He did not roll his eyes in a "there-goes-the-neighborhood" moment of disdain. He did not make it known that he would be watching me and send me a silent signal of distrust. Just a smile and a wave. I made plans to get up early in the morning to go sit on his porch and talk with him, and maybe meet the person who delivers our newspapers. The journey of life had led me to a new reality, slowing me down as I saw with open eyes the beauty of its simplicity.

I never feel more at peace in my neighborhood than when I hear the thunder and see the rain. The economic landscape here could scare you, but we are on a hill, where it never floods. Despite the gritty questions and hard answers found on my street, rain does not discriminate, and the God who pours it out does not love another part of town more than this one. I know that it is falling on my former Meadowgreen roof and on this one both the same. Thunder doesn't acknowledge city limits or determine which side of the railroad tracks will have their windows shaken, and the God who unleashes it wants all ears to hear him. I may think that I see signs of his favor only in other places, but my will has lousy eyesight. His ways, which are not my ways, are always perfect. The thunder and rain say that we are part of his world, and when the sun comes out we'll do what we have to do to make it better. Life is wherever his gospel can be heard, and hell is anywhere that he is not.

And Hard Bargain is home.

9   God's Neighborhood

THE NEWSPAPERS PILED UP, LEANING LIKE THE TOWER OF PISA, held down by a block of wood keeping them from flying away. They represented several weeks' source of heat for William Murry and combined with whatever sticks, cut logs, and burnable products he collected, the periodicals were his connection to a better understanding of world news before combustion and a warmer quality of life after. My two sons weekly contributed our family's small offering of newspapers, magazines and papers suitable for burning.

Neighborly care, friendship and love seem to be the essence of biblical faith. William and Katie watch our house when we are away. They are true caregivers growing older along with the neighborhood. Because of lack of mobility they really know about the comings and goings on Glass Street. The power of the gospel is demonstrated to us through our neighbors. God uses William and Katie in our poverty of surveillance. My sons care for the Murrys' poverty of fuel.

All of our poverty is represented in the one most crucial need of salvation from the realities of hell, separating us from our life-giving Creator. Jesus identified with our poverty. He came to earth, relocating from heaven, taking on human flesh. In his birth, life and death he demonstrated poverty. His parents, Mary and Joseph, were poor. His job as a carpenter was considered vocationally to be at the level of the working poor. His death on the cross was the execution of a criminal reserved for the lowest of class distinctions, and his burial as a victim of Roman crucifixion couldn't be a clearer sign of his intentionally coming for those who despair, are disinherited, orphaned, lonely, lost and therefore poor.

To understand service to each other as actual service to God is a freeing realization. Jesus came to serve; we therefore serve one another as service to him. Then we do all of it together to demonstrate the power of the gospel uniting God's people—seeing unity in Jesus as the method the Lord uses to accomplish his will in caring for the poor.

Ephesians 4:2-6 reminds us of this celebration of diversity in Jesus. We are called to be *one!* This translates as a partnership with those in our neighborhoods and communities who, back and forth, help each other succeed in meeting the needs of the poor. Reinforcing the biblical ideal of relationship-based development rather than program-based development is Jesus' mandate in John 13:34-35, where he commands us to love one another. This mandate is reflected as the basis for all Maundy Thursday celebrations in the church's Holy Week services and is clearly the operation motto for Christ's disciples. We love each other and especially the poor. A loveless Christian is an oxymoron. A merciless Christian is a non sequitur. A Christian who does not serve the poor represents a total biblical contradiction.

These opportunities arise daily in Hard Bargain. William's daughter came to our door one day to tell us her daddy had been robbed. She told me a well-dressed African American man came to her parents' door telling convincing lies, leading William to hand over five thousand dollars in cash, the total of his life savings. Police were notified, but the thief was never caught. The story got out to the local media, and money began to roll in from strangers: one check for $1,100, another for $100 and gifts of cash. The surrounding community of Franklin and Nashville helped to meet the immediate need of Hard Bargain patriarch William Murry.

Isaiah's prophecy tells how God's Messiah will not break a tender shoot or blow out the smoldering wick. We are to love with that same tenderness and fan into flame the heart for God in those close to us, gently leading and caring with dignity, justice and true Christlike love. Micah called to God's people to see our world through the eyes of compassion because the Lord has shown us what is good and how he requires his children to live. He says we must act justly, love mercy and walk humbly with God.

Another of the countless biblical principles teaching us how to care for the poor is that of *vision*. Jesus always kept the vision of his kingdom's mission in the forefront of his mind and actions. We are required to do that as well! We are distracted often by the peripheral callings demanding our attention and rising up to beg to be our priority. We must resist the temptation to lay down the larger purpose to pick up a smaller, more immediate one. As it turns out, most immediate needs are met as a result of sticking to the original vision and calling.

In John 6:14-15, we see Jesus being called out by the crowds to become the King and continue as the miracle worker because he had just done something spectacular to help the people. He had fed several thousand of them in a miraculous way. It seemed to all that, whatever Israel was looking for, this must be it, and they were willing to be his loyal subjects if he could keep up that kind of behavior! He didn't flinch. He got in his boat and took off. He knew his mission and where he was headed. He knew he came for the cross, and aren't we glad he kept on task! Can we see by Jesus' example how we must act in caring for the poor? We have a great vision of God's kingdom ahead of us. So we must resist the various competing voices to follow that calling!

Several examples of how these principles work have been lived out in front of us. Let me introduce you to two families who have demonstrated courage and godly resolve. They did not let the plague of poverty devour them, but rather stuck with whatever resources the Lord provided, contributing to and functioning in God's kingdom's work to care for the poor.

We begin with a young lady who was a teenage student when we first met. She had been living in under-managed housing with her drug-addicted single mother and two younger siblings for several years. Paige Overton had befriended her in the neighborhood, and the young woman responded to various invitations to join programs offered through Franklin Community Ministries. Their relationship today spans more than ten years of growing together and ministering to each other. It has been inspiring to watch this young woman's life go from having no future to personal victory, where she models how God takes people out of hopeless situations and rescues them in the gospel.

The young woman, Tyheesia Esmond, is married to Rod Esmond, a young man who has been in relationship with mentors and disciplers in the Empty Hands Fellowship. They have three beautiful children, and they live across the road from us on Glass Street in Hard Bargain in a rehabbed transitional home we call the Carrie Wilson House. The house is named for a prominent Hard Bargain citizen who gave fifty-plus years of service as a teacher in the Williamson County school system.

Tyheesia has been the assistant coordinator of the Store House Ministry under FCM and served in the offices at the Franklin Com-

Tyheesia Esmond (left) and her son Xavier, with Paige Overton Pitts.

munity Center on the corner of Third Avenue and Church Street. In that
role she worked daily with walk-up clients, some with needs easily met
and others with seemingly insurmountable problems. She is a great listener and compassionate caretaker of her friends and neighbors.

Tyheesia's three children are enrolled at New Hope Academy. Her
mother is also a true hero, as she battled and won an aggressive fight
with drug addiction. She is over at the house quite often and is contributing financial resources to her children and precious grandchildren. Tyheesia's brother is a star athlete at the local high school, and
her sister is a beautiful teenager growing in grace and mercy each day
as the gospel is lived out among her family. For every one person like
Tyheesia, however, there are 100 who unfortunately do not make it.
Again, if our goal was to see people live up to our expectations, it
would not be a gospel approach. All we can do is love. The results are
always up to God.

Another example of how the gospel has been demonstrated in our community is the life of Valery Caldwell. She is an African American woman, a single mom with three beautiful kids, one with extreme special needs. Valery started out in the worst public housing complex in Williamson County and is now the proud owner of her own home, built by a coalition of friends and family through the Williamson County Habitat for Humanity.

Valery was first introduced to FCM by Cady Wilson, the current director, who at the time ran the Eagles program caring for elementary-aged public school children in need of tutoring and mentoring. After knocking on Valery's door, Cady kept up the relationship, and they both found a lifetime friendship. Recently Cady served as Valery's matron of honor in her wedding.

Valery, armed with a high school diploma, worked her way through a rigorous Bachelor of Science program in Social Work at Tennessee State University, graduating high in her class with a degree and an opportunity to get out of public housing. She was a Welfare to Work mother of three and one of the most courageous and determined young women I know. She eventually attended the community church's Tuesday morning Bible study taught by Pastor Scotty Smith and was discipled in the gospel through that time in the Word.

Franklin Community Ministries hired her to direct the Storehouse Ministry, and only recently she left to seek a better-paying job with the Tennessee Department of Human Services. She was and is a tremendous resource for the needy in our city and county. Her story shows the strength of relationships through hard times and better times and demonstrates that anything is possible in the Lord if none of us care who gets the credit.

God's neighborhoods are connected to form communities and cities. One of my favorite passages of Scripture is 2 Kings 2:19-22. It's about a poisoned river flowing through the city of Jericho, which the prophet Elisha cleansed by pouring salt into, a process that left the river never to be poisoned again. Sound familiar? Jesus our perfect prophet cleanses the river of sin and hopelessness. He uses the salt and light that each of his children display as they live out the gospel of his grace and mercy, declaring the Savior's love, a love that will never let go! The river is clean!

One of the popular sayings in our community is that when a brokenhearted, weak, wasted person floats by us on that river we must reach in and rescue them, helping them to a shore that they could not see or find because of their lostness. The analogy, however, does not end there. In fact, Christian community demands that we not only care for those floating by in deep need, but that we head upstream and find out why they are "falling in" in the first place, or investigate who is pushing them in.

Christian community development is both the existential work of finding a way to help here and now and the proactive work of healing the source of the problems. To be effective in this kind of ministry, you must be willing to evaluate and reevaluate your mission. Are you keeping to the vision? Are you trusting in Jesus by faith through his Spirit of love and mercy? Do the Scriptures regulate your efforts? Is it about both words and deeds? Ecclesiastes 3:1 reminds us that everything under God's heaven has a season. We must apply that teaching to our Christian community development. What is Jesus doing? If we know, let's go forward in faith to accomplish that. If we don't know, let's not pretend we do, but rather stop, pray and wait on the Lord!

RACIALIZATION

We've looked at basic biblical teaching on care for the poor in God's neighborhood. For the rest of this chapter I would like to take a specific look at the scriptural call to racial reconciliation. We've seen through Jesus' example that relocation and creative reneighboring are important to the ministry of mercy and that empowerment of disinherited people like Valery or Tyheesia is clearly an answer to the call for biblical justice. Racial reconciliation is perhaps the most vital of all forms of renewal for a new Franklin and a new South. What does the Bible say about race, ethnicity, and our coming together to advance his kingdom? When men and women in the South cross over racial, economic and denominational divides to work together in relationships that encourage caring for one another, it is truly a miraculous demonstration of the Gospel.

Although there have been great strides in our country there is still a race problem. In a wonderful book titled *Divided by Faith: Evangelical Religion and the Problem of Race in America*, authors Michael O. Emerson and Christian Smith define their word *racialization*. It seems that many of us can't take the idea of being called racist, but being called racialized is somehow acceptable. Listen to what Emerson and Smith are saying.

> The definition of racialization is an understanding that racial practices that reproduce racial divisions in the contemporary United States: (1) are increasingly covert, (2) are embedded in the normal operations of institutions, (3) avoid direct racial terminology, and are invisible to most whites. It [racialization] understands that racism is not mere individual overt prejudice or the free-floating irrational driver of race problems, but the collective misuse of power that results in diminished life opportunities for some racial groups. Racism is a changing ideology with the constant and rational purpose of perpetuating and justifying a social system that is racialized. The justification may

include overt prejudice and discrimination, but these are not necessary. Because racialization is embedded within the normal, everyday operations of institutions, this framework understands that people need not intend their actions to contribute to racial division and inequality for their actions to do so.[1]

As Denny Denson and I began teaching the "Introduction to Sociology" class at the Nashville Technical College, we were overwhelmed with questions about race relations in the South. Students wanted to know how they could help change things from the way they've always been to a new southern attitude more in line with their progressive, somewhat colorblind, idealism.

Denny and I pointed out that we don't want to be color blind, although we know the heart behind that statement desires to see all people as equal and therefore the same. What we truly desire is to clearly see our differences as something to be celebrated. Color is good, and the more color in our lives, the better off we are. We explained to the students that relationships represent the doorway to the new South. It is through intentional friendship-building or creative and connectional reneighboring that we move forward in trust. Denny Denson and I often vote differently and see many issues from opposite sides of priorities. But being able to commit ourselves to each other, no matter how much disagreement we have, allows for the kind of honest conflict that breeds true intimacy and sets reconciliation free to do its thing.

Remember, Denny is an African American from a ghetto on the south side of Chicago, a Vietnam veteran and a former soldier in the militant Black Panther Party. He is a tough guy. I, on the other hand, am a white middle-class kid from northern Virginia who spent summers at the country club, am an Eagle Scout, lived a private-prep-school privileged lifestyle (relatively speaking). I'm an easygoing, nice guy. We were as compatible as oil and water, yet with God's grace and mercy we've become best of friends and brothers who would willingly die for each other.

Any time we talk to groups or individuals about racial reconciliation we share what we feel the Bible has to say. This isn't about Denny Denson's and Scott Roley's concepts. It is about interpreting the Scriptures to find a way to live out reconciliation with God and with each other. Today's church remains racially separated, and we feel that is sin. The quote on racialization from Emerson and Smith reminds us that current struggles are very similar to the racial trials that plagued the church in biblical times. Jewish and Gentile separation was everywhere, and that was an ethnic problem. The apostles Paul and Peter battled over taking the gospel across national divides. When redemption is looked at as a huge heavenly host filled with members from *every* tribe, tongue and people group, that is racial reconciliation at its best! So, the case for biblical racial reconciliation is not the product of a simple prooftext or two. It is an overwhelming confirmation that God in Scripture has given us principles leading us to worship him by reconciling our racial hatred and bias. His forgiveness leads us to repentance!

British theologian John Stott has been very helpful in organizing principles for racial reconciliation from Scripture. One of the first principles I want to highlight is the biblical teaching that there is unity in the human race. We are all created by the same God who continues to be involved in each one of our lives. Acts 17:24-25 tells us that God is the Creator of all things, which causes us to rejoice, knowing we are in some way organically attached to every other people group on the earth. Because this is true, another principle becomes apparent and that is to applaud the obvious diversity of ethnic cultures. We are one race with lots of ethnicity. To affirm the diversity of ethnic cultures sets us free from the temptation to judge our culture as God's one and only group. Again, Acts 17:26-28 goes on to reinforce this understanding. God is the Lord of history. He made it that way for a purpose, and we need to accept the greatness of God-given ethnicity. If we look to the final picture of heaven in Revelation 7:9 and following, it is a clear vision of unity in the midst of diversity.

In the Lord's Prayer Jesus teaches us to pray "on earth as it is in heaven." That would seem to reinforce the celebration of our diversity as the people of God and the picture of all of us together eternally worshiping our creative God.

Continuing in Acts 17:30-31, we are taught that God has revealed his son Jesus as the only way, truth and life. Jesus is the only Savior. This exclusivity makes it clear that ethnic pluralism is right and good, but there is no room for religious pluralism. God as the God of Revelation points only to Jesus and is going to judge every one of us, every ethnic group and every race based on our response to the revelation of Jesus Christ.

Because each person is judged equally on his or her response to Jesus, and we know cultural pluralism is a good thing from God's hand, we can also deduce that the plurality of religions and so called "alternate" ways of salvation stand in opposition to God's revealed Messiah, Jesus. Let me once again make this point as clear as possible: There is no other way to heaven. The entire canon of Scripture is set on this. "There is no other name under heaven given to men" and the perfect words of our Lord and Savior Jesus: "I am the way and the truth and the life. No one comes to the Father except through me" (Acts 4:12; John 14:6).

John Stott sums up this idea, presenting God as the God of all redemption: "Galatians 3, verse 28 tells us that Jesus died and rose again to create a new and reconciled community. This reconciliation is both vertical and horizontal. The New Testament (particularly the book of Acts) is the record of this ingathering of nations into a single community of faith. God does not consider ethnicity when he re-deems. Instead, he brings people from every tribe and nation into his household of faith based on his own mercy. Thus, while we do have racial distinctions, these no longer divide us because we have a deeper unity in common redemption."[2]

Denny Denson finishes our time of teaching about racial reconcil-iation by reminding the audience who we are in Jesus. He alone is the reconciler we desire to know. The good news is Jesus does it perfectly, and those who believe in him are in union with him. You might po-litically be a Republican concentrating on correcting depravity in each individual's failure to respond to the current American dream. You might be a Democrat who fights the public and private oppres-sion that stabs at the heart of those attempting to rise up and make it on their own. Biblical social justice for Denny and me is the surren-dering of self-serving ideologies to see that oppression and individual depravity both exist and that Republican and Democrat alike are headed down the same path without the love of Jesus.

Denny and I are different. We do almost everything differently. He is the pastor of First Missionary Baptist Church, the "gateway to the ghetto" (Denny's term), and at the same time he lives in the suburbs. I am a pastor at a church in the suburbs, Christ Community Church, which is a large Presbyterian Church in America (PCA) church in a very nice area of Franklin, Tennessee, and I live in the "hood." We have both lived in the northern United States, and we have both lived in the southern United States, and now Franklin is our home until Jesus moves us elsewhere.

Our story is one of pride, foolishness and forgiveness. We are committing ourselves to each other and to creative and connectional forms of reneighboring so that we will always be among the poor. We also pledge to work together empowering the disinherited people all around us. I pray for and help Denny with his ministry to young men who battle drug abuse. He has helped me with my special projects, like recently challenging the denomination I'm a member of to repent and apologize for the southern Presbyterian Church's role in justifying the North Atlantic slave trade and the 150 years of silence that we are guilty of. His prayers and support are what keep me going, and I'm sure he would say the same about me.

We agree that we have a long way to go in our growth in racial reconciliation. There was a time when neither of us thought about it at all. It is in God's hands that each person comes to see the reasons for racial reconciliation in her or his own time. We are all in process and need to be encouraged wherever we are in the racial reconciliation continuum. As I reflect on my own journey along that continuum, I can see how far I have to go and thank the Lord for how far he has brought me. The inspiration and vision planted in my young soul as I witnessed the summer of '63 led me to look for a philosophy of life or a worldview that was consistent with what I heard from King and Kennedy, namely walk your talk.

It was in Christianity that I found the mandate for all of life being subject to God's reign and rule. *Coram Deo*, God over all creation, meant that "care for the poor" wasn't just a catch phrase. It was clear from Scripture that because the Lord's calling to his people is both in word and deed, then to accomplish his will I could expect the community of Christ's people to give to and serve the less fortunate.

In my classroom teaching through the church, I often finish my time of sharing with the phrase, "get out there and make a mess." It seems appropriate for Christians to be wide open and free-wheeling. All things are permissible, but not all things are profitable. Scripture forms a basis for Christian ethics. The law of love demands we care for others as radically as we care for ourselves, so we should be off the charts with love for the least and the lost. The biblical world and life view is anchored in Jesus' declaring God to be the Creator over all and in understanding his love for his creation. The severity of loss in the Fall of humanity and the depth, width, height and breadth of Jesus' redemption seeking his chosen ones as far as the curse is found leads us full force into the messy adventure. Every moment of a Christian's life is raging both with the powerful turmoil of sin and the amazing truth of God's love. The peace in God's neighborhood is more secure through the discovery of our passion to see things change.

One of my passions is fly fishing. There really isn't anything that refreshes my soul like standing knee-deep in a trout stream in some beautiful place casting to wily fish. The intrigue, grace, challenge, glory, joy, effort, struggle, anticipation, humiliation, fun and peace that go with this sport are reasons enough for me to go back to the river. When Middle Tennessee tail water forfeits an eighteen-inch rainbow trout, the feeling is like God has leaned over and kissed me.

As I rest and find my soul's peace in the midst of the river, I am reminded of God's grace and mercy. It makes me ponder the depth of his love for me and his creation. In the river I meet the one who entered the river for me, was baptized into life, then died and was raised to eternal life as God and King. I am in union with this one, this Jesus, the Baptizer, the Reconciler, and the one who came to dwell among us, relocating from heaven to earth. He reconciles us through his blood shed on the cross, a death substituted for the death I deserve, his life and righteousness credited to me, a righteousness I could never attain.

Maybe the river remains my refuge because its constant movement is like life: always processing, always wild, within its defined banks ready to burst forth and create new ones or just sink deep into the channel where the torrent's clarity and purity miraculously carry away the pain.

In Hard Bargain are the weak, the forgotten, and the drowned souls of our bias, hatred, prejudice and fear. Jesus is the shalom of the city. He lifts us all. He carries and saves us. His rescue is forever. When the day is done and, like William Murry, we are being warmed by the fires of our homes, maybe we'll see God's grace even more as we close our eyes and greet him in the midst of his embrace, true peace in the neighborhood of God.

10   Repentance

I LOOKED AT SCOTTY AND HE LOOKED BACK AT ME WITH THAT
"can you believe we just heard what was said?" look. We've shared
that look many times before just as brothers share an old ball glove
or a "cool" shirt. This time, though, it seemed disheartening to think
we both had to listen to the protectors of dominant culture religion
state their case once more. What was hard for us to hear was the renewal of the myth that we, the white people, really are smarter and
certainly more in God's favor than people who are not white, not like
us. What Scott Ward Smith and I were doing in that room was trying
to convince a group of Christian elders to consider the idea of our
dominant culture denomination actually repenting for and offering
apology to those with ancestors offended and brutalized by the North
Atlantic slave trade. This offering was nothing more than a bridge for
us all to walk over in order to extend a hand of fellowship and love
to our African American brothers and sisters.

Why is it so hard to say "I'm sorry," or "we're sorry," or "we were
wrong"? Nothing can excuse what our forefathers did, and the results
of their actions have wrecked our relational reality. We have perpet-

uated the myth of white supremacy by not talking about it, not confessing it, being stubborn about facing it, and the result is that we spread the myth all the more. If a white person's daughter falls in love and marries a black person's son it's too bad for them. Why? Because they both aren't white people? Most would say, "Well, if they were both black people it would be better," but still the majority of dominant culture people feel it is better to be a white person, better to be born in a white nation with a white heritage.

For me and the denomination I belong to, there is great pride in the work done by God providentially through the seventeenth-century Protestant reformers. The development of the New World and specifically the Euro-dominated North American continent is celebrated as the flower of biblical religion. What happens so often is that European or white-dominant-culture-defined Western civilization, which has clearly given so much to the world, is considered "better"—better than Eastern or Asian culture, African culture, Caribbean Rim, Central (Latino) and South American (Hispanic) culture, Native North American or First Nations culture, and any other forgotten, ethnically different way of life.

The idea of Western civilization being better is a simple value judgment settled on because of advancements in a number of disciplines and is the root of the myth of white supremacy. Dominant-culture white people in North America believe that because the Eurocentric aspect of our society remains in place, it therefore is *superior* to any other rival cultural contenders. Because white culture is better, therefore white people are better. The American dream is that poor people have the chance to get rich and contribute to society. Nobody is denied access, and the way is equally open to every individual. To get there simply takes hard work.

Obviously, the dominant culture defines and determines what success really is and what contributions are valuable. If the myth is believed, it is easy to see how whiteness is taught to be better than non-whiteness. For the church, the idea of one civilization being better than another is a problem in God's eyes, continually contributing to the myth of white supremacy. Being a great civilization, performing wonderful moral acts, and contributing to the advancement of education, health, safety and religion are all tremendous accomplishments and should be applauded. The problem is that all of those beautiful things are *not* Christianity.

To confuse Western civilization, the American Dream, the Protestant Reformation, Western Roman Catholicism, Eastern Orthodoxy and so on with the exclusive version of biblical Christianity is a huge sin indeed. To say that biblical Christianity is found to some degree in each of those events and institutions is good and right. But the Scriptures do not elevate any time period or civilization. What is elevated is the cross of Jesus where every nation, tribe, tongue and people group are welcomed. Let us always remember Jesus was not white. As missions expert Ray Bakke[1] reminds us, Jesus was a Middle-Eastern Jewish person who in truth was Asian born and soon after became a refugee in North Africa.

Has God used the Western European nations over the past five hundred years to do good? Absolutely! Has the dominant culture of North America overstepped God-given authority and leadership, sinning against God and his plan for unity? Again, absolutely.

Sixteenth-century West African culture was essentially kidnapped and brought to the New World through, by some estimates, 20 to 40 million people who endured 350 years of slavery. The North Atlantic slave trade was extremely brutal. Not only was the North Atlantic slave trade route farther and more physically demanding, but the myth of white superiority reigned in the Western European colonial culture, and the young North American colonies believed it tena-ciously and held onto it like it was written by God on stone tablets.

Assimilation of Africans in the South and Central American conti-nents with Native American peoples and Euro-colonists was more successful than efforts in the North Atlantic. The severity of treatment given first to the native North Americans and then to the kidnapped African Americans shows the sense of superiority in the dominant cul-ture. In the southern United States, especially, assimilation has been slow. The nineteenth-century war, emancipation and one hundred years of enduring invisible Jim Crow laws leading to the second eman-cipation with the Civil Rights Act of the 1960s is the historical back-drop to the almost impossible job of dismantling the myth.

European-dominated culture is a wonderful thing, but when it is promoted as superior and its people as superior beings, its beauty turns into a foulness only the love of God can challenge and change. The myth holds that the self-proclaimed beautiful people are the bet-ter people.

I stood helpless behind the young Mexican who was trying to pay for the gasoline he had just pumped into the aging faded red pickup truck. It was overloaded with other Spanish-speaking men ready to head out to work either as day laborers on some kind of construction job or in fields as farm hands helping to produce a harvest on the vast portions of land that still represent 60 percent of Williamson County. The attendant at the counter was screaming at the young man, de-manding that he communicate in English, which of course was an ac-ceptable desire. But his being so angry and out of control reinforced what I found out later. The white man at the counter hated Mexican people. He felt that theirs was an inferior culture and they were infe-rior as people. I wished I spoke Spanish so I could translate into Eng-lish a defense of the young man who was clearly upset and frustrated by simply trying to pay the right amount of money and who wanted to get away from that scene as quickly as possible.

It is clear that a loving act toward the growing minority cultures of North America would be to learn the language of the group most dominant in your area. Spanish, Creole, Chinese, Portuguese, French, etc., are all tongues that would be valuable to speak. Perhaps we might consider learning another language as a challenge preparing us to love better. Could it be that God wants his people undertaking a linguistic study as an act done for the "least of these"? And therefore any act done to the least of these is one done unto him.

A biblical world and life view that allows us to see creation, fall and redemption in the context of culture and ethnicity sets us free to celebrate the great heritage that underlies Western culture. The Protestant Reformation and its massive creedal contributions to discipling the body of Christ to "think Christianly" and to "act Christianly" offer the ultimate goal of culture and reasons for ethnicity. The teaching is in the form of questions and answers. "What is the chief end of Man?" is the opening question of the shorter Catechism. The answer is "To glorify God and enjoy him forever." This biblical answer for God's people helps us battle the self-serving temptations of the cultural myths.

Glorifying God in caring for the poor, especially through empowering disinherited people, is to really see Jesus at work, correcting the wrongs done in the name of a superior-acting culture, and bringing justice out of the oppression so many who are dismissed by its tyranny feel. The essence of creedal Christianity is in shrinking down the great big ideas to help us to grow in grace and mercy. We find God's glory in loving those who are very different from ourselves and the true joy of being with Jesus, which blows away the prejudices and fears.

In the mid-1960s, I had to have vaccinations against nearly every known disease contracted by mankind when I signed up for simple sailing lessons at the National Marina on the Virginia side of the Potomac River across from Washington, D.C. The Potomac was so polluted at that time that it smelled much like a freshly opened can of motor oil. The chunks of stuff floating everywhere looked like giant croutons in the cream-colored waters that reminded me of the foamy head lifting itself up out of a pint of Guinness. I was there to master the art of sailing. I wanted to have fun; most of those in my class wanted to win races. We banged around in twelve-foot boats called jets and small rowboat-styled nutshells rigged for sailing. We learned not to jibe, but rather the proper techniques for coming about and the definitions of nautical terms such as rudder, centerboard, sheet, jib, spinnaker, port, starboard, fore and aft, and so on.

The snooty sailing crowd I was thrown in with created tension because of my newly formed sixth-grade view of social justice and care for the poor. The future lessons learned at the sailing marina, like those learned from charging my lunches at the Woodlawn Country Club snack bar, were that privileged people have a responsibility: "To those that much is given, much is required," the Scripture tells us. What the American dream and the preferential myths sometimes create is a lifestyle where the whole deal is about the individual. We forget about the community. I fell into a dream world as a country-club kid, private Episcopalian, middle-school brat and self-envisioned playboy sailor spending winters in Bermuda and wasting away in Hamilton Harbor barrooms. None of that was ever going to happen because my family was always there pointing me to a mirror, busting my chops. However, just tasting the life of "the haves" helped me see there really is a life of the "have-nots."

What I was discovering was the painfully obvious truth that confusing the American Dream with true Christianity plagued God's people in North America and especially those living in the South. In 1986, when my family and our small fellowship of developers expanded our ministries into the wealthy city of Franklin, Tennessee, the contrast of the haves and have-nots came back into view. The church, just like secular society, had seemingly bought into the myth of white supremacy. Realizing that dilemma helped us repent and respond to God's call to care for the poor.

As my family made decisions that led us away from the neighborhoods of the privileged middle class, it was not to be martyrs or self-proclaimed leaders. It was because we felt the call to live among poor people. We were searching for creative ways of reneighboring, or living together with the poorest of the poor. Poverty and race relations were connected in Franklin, as they are all over the United States where a large percentage of the poor are minorities. The loving relationships Jesus brought to us were the tools used in the hands of the Lord to fashion a better way as the small community of harvesters battled the abuses of the American dream.

Patterns of championing the elite might also be revealed in our obsessions over youth, beauty, strength, speed, power, riches and so on. As Tim Keller says, in the gospel is the truth that gives power to the believer to substitute insecurities with boldness and arrogance with humility. A secular Western civilization world and life view, which even in the minds of some believers is elevated beyond a biblical world and life view, creates the temptation to fall for the seductive wooing in those patterns. It obscures the great paradoxes of life. To those caught in the magnetic beam of the myth there is no tension between wealthy and poor, weakness and strength, the American dream and biblical faith.

As we fought the unending battle to free ourselves from the power of those misleading notions, we became more aware of the issues of poverty plaguing our city. We realized that from our historic and orthodox Christian roots there had formed a biblical platform sturdy enough to launch revivals of mercy and racial reconciliation in our town. However, too few candidates appeared willing to climb on board the rocket and blast off. It looked like the process was going to be more like a slow-moving train.

Maybe what was happening to us was a conversion of sorts—a desire to see what might happen in our town where the beauty of the South and the light of American abundance was shining brightly. Maybe there would be change as radical as the myth of white supremacy dying and the real truth of Christ's supremacy being resurrected, bringing glory to God and joy to his people.

In a city where the centerpiece on the town square is the statue of a rebel soldier on a pedestal twenty feet high, could it be possible that Christ would replace that icon with the image of his cross, proving him to be the ultimate rebel? A rebel so radical that he refused to bow to the myths of beauty and ethnicity, refused to give in to the power structures and political pressure of his time. Through faith in him we found the same freedom to do what he commanded: to care for the poor through racial reconciliation, creative and connectional re-neighboring, and the empowerment of disinherited people.

Empowerment to a human being is the idea that someone can be given the opportunity to fulfill a calling. It's ultimately a desire to see Jesus save an individual and be there as the person's sufficiency and strength.

OVERTURE TWENTY

I arrived back in Franklin at 3:30 p.m. that Thursday after Scotty and I met with that group of elders. I was on my cell phone with Scotty, standing in the front yard of my house on Glass Street in Hard Bargain. He was describing the scene on the floor of the PCA's General Assembly back in Birmingham, Alabama, where I had been with him four hours earlier. I was forced to leave the General Assembly before its conclusion to get my son Jeff back for a youth missions-trip meeting. Scotty's words broke through the bad connection, "It's an overwhelming majority in favor of the overture and the commissioners are standing and clapping in worship!" I just held on to the phone, listening silently, and weeping.

One year earlier I had passed a note to Charles McGowan with the question of how a commissioner submits a personal resolution to the General Assembly to get it into the permanent record. We were in Dallas, Texas, at that year's General Assembly and Dr. McGowan, who was the pastor of Christ Presbyterian Church in Nashville, Tennessee, responded by asking me what my resolution was. I handed him what I had jotted down—a crude statement of repentance and apology by the PCA for their role in continuing to ignore what the southern Presbyterian Church had promoted in supporting southern chattel slavery and in establishing churches which discriminated against certain members based on race. I had scribbled the simple statement at my desk in Franklin several months earlier. Charles read the memo and said, "Let's talk." I stuffed the crumpled paper in my pocket and took it out a week later when we got back home. Dr. McGowan suggested I rewrite it and give it to the Christ Community Church session for approval. We could then take it to the Nashville Presbytery and, if it passed there, send it on as an official overture to the General Assembly meeting that June in Birmingham, Alabama.

The significance of the apology coming there was important historically, and it seemed the timing could be right. I immediately sent my inarticulate scrawl to Dr. George Grant, a marvelous writer with grace and style. He put the *whereases* and *therefores* together, and we gave it to the pastors and elders of the Christ Community Church session. After good counsel and wise suggestions it was carried to the Nashville Presbytery where it was unanimously passed, which came as a shock to me.

The members of the Presbytery agreed to send it on as an overture to be debated and voted on at the General Assembly. So, later that June in Birmingham, the Bills and Overtures Committee of the GA did its work on the overture along with other similar overtures, trying to determine what course of action best represented the will of the PCA. Certain language was too inflammatory, and some absolutely rejected the idea of our repenting for the sins of slavery because we were not there to commit them. There was another deep concern that if this debate turned ugly, it would show our minority members just how racialized the denomination was, as if they didn't already know, and put our movement for crosscultural ministry back, maybe for good.

As the week went on and the room where the Bills and Overtures Committee met filled up with elders curious about the debate, many courageous members took a stand on the issue. Thaddeus (Cal) Borroughs did the final tweaking on what has become known as Overture 20, and after being accepted in committee it was scheduled for debate on the floor. The big moment came late in the afternoon on Thursday and no one really knew what would happen. Providentially, the Lord found favor with Overture 20, and it became a little stone in a little sling. As I stood in my yard in Hard Bargain weeping, I realized I was crying over the goodness of the God of grace who destroyed his only Son in our place. We are all racists and self-infatuated sinners who deserve his wrath. Instead he gives us freedom to repent, receive and give mercy, and live our lives in service as wor-

ship to our loving and forgiving God. Following is the overture that
was presented in Birmingham.

> Whereas the heinous sins attendant with the unbiblical forms
> of servitude—including oppression, racism, exploitation,
> man-stealing, and chattel slavery—stand in opposition to the
> gospel; and,
>
> Whereas the effects of these sins have created and continue
> to create barriers between brothers and sisters of different races
> and/or economic spheres; and,
>
> Whereas the aftereffects of these sins continue to be felt in the
> economic, cultural, and social affairs of the communities in
> which we live and minister;
>
> We therefore confess our involvement in these sins. As a peo-
> ple, both we and our fathers, have failed to keep the command-
> ments, the statutes, and the laws God has commanded. We
> therefore publicly repent of our pride, our complacency, and
> our complicity. Furthermore, we seek the forgiveness of our
> brothers and sisters for the reticence of our hearts that have
> constrained us from acting swiftly in the matter.
>
> We will strive, in a manner consistent with the gospel imper-
> atives, for the encouragement of racial reconciliation, the estab-
> lishment of urban and minority congregations, and the en-
> hancement of existing ministries of mercy in our cities, among
> the poor, and across all social, racial, and economic boundaries,
> to the glory of God.

The results of Overture 20 were in God's hands. What has happened since has been the writing of another overture as a rationalization to encourage the brightest and best minds of the PCA to com-
pose a Pastoral Position Paper discussing race and the gospel. The

ultimate goal is to see the PCA reach out across racial, cultural and economic divides to build a denomination committing itself to seeing the gospel drive our fulfillment of Jesus' great commission.

The PCA has been notoriously wealthy, white and well educated. The development of minority leadership is clearly a next step in putting together congregations that reflect the true bride of Christ. Without minority leaders there would be no future for the PCA, at least not one of significance. Without cross cultural development the PCA would be in danger of staying the way it was: no change of heart, no change in the people, no change in the culture. As in all of North America, if we don't embrace and work with minorities in our southern institutions, the new South will not emerge. God have mercy on us and bring the light of Christ to lead us.

Little stones in little slings can bring down the mightiest of giants, and in Birmingham that June at least a small giant was slain. With my son Jeff at my side, I was able to watch the dismantling of my own heart and its dead systems. I felt like I was set free from living like a lifeless monument to dead orthodoxy, unable to respond to the poison choking its people. I was serving a church led by great minds, with hearts in need of revival. The monuments needed life. The reformation needed reforming. I was its biggest problem, full of self-righteous answers and ideas. Through Overture 20 I was able to witness the beginning of the death of my hypocrisy, foolishness and ignorance that I'm sure will take a lifetime to purge.

CHRIST OUR SUBSTITUTE

Critical to reconciliation are Jesus' substitution for his children by dying on the cross for them and the substitution of his righteousness based on his living a perfect life. His baptism by John the Baptist showed Jesus' heart for repentance even though he was innocent of sin.

The water was cold as it hit Jesus' head and shoulders. It startled him and brought the same awakening of heart, lungs and spirit in him as it did for you and me the moment we were baptized. Jesus' submission to John's baptism was for the forgiveness of sins not committed by him. He identified with his followers who did sin.

My knee had been obliterated by a 250-pound linebacker when I tried unsuccessfully to turn the right end of the DePauw University offensive line. The injury ended my football career. Six months later, the bad knee hindered my ability to stand in the somewhat rough Pacific Ocean surf pounding the peninsula south of San Francisco on the California coast. The day I was baptized I was propped up by two Christian brothers willing to risk their lives for my sake. They allowed me to collapse into the brine for the pronouncement and administration of the Trinitarian sacrament. With their strong arms they lifted me to the fresh sea air filling my lungs as I sputtered and squawked out praise to God.

The baptism of Jesus was probably safer and more decent. It wasn't any less a human experience celebrating what God had done. Jesus cares for broken, weak, limping, poor creatures like me and you. Jesus in the Jordan River was reason enough for me to wade in after him, seeking glorious results through similar motives, desiring to meet the needs of the poor by entering their lives in a down to earth way. The love of God, which motivates us, is the love Jesus shares with the Father. The overflow of that love, mercy and grace spills out to everyone we come in contact with.

In concluding this chapter I want to draw attention to the history of our racialized society. Some historians estimate that 25 million or more black people were kidnapped from West Africa and brought to the North, Central and South American continents over a 350-year period. The long distance and violent northern weather made the passage to the region, first to the emerging colonies and then to the sovereign nation, the most brutal route of all the slave trade. It seems that genocide, holocaust, and mass murder, whenever found in history, should be defined by this most heinous of crimes. The number of dead is impossible to estimate. The entire loss of heritage, family, homeland and culture for such a mass of people should shock and stretch our imaginations. When I think of it I hold my head in my hands in amazement or denial like I do when realizing the rings of Saturn are real. Maybe the shock of it is tied up with the spin we put on it. Like Saturn's rings held in place by gravity, we hold on to ideas that help us live with ourselves. We welcome images of black people just hanging around the North American continent like Native Americans or European colonists—nice ideas to make us feel good, as in a mirage. They look like something they are not. We must test them, throw rocks at them, and see they are not real. We can't imagine the slave trade was actually true.

Assimilation of Africans in South America, Central America and the Caribbean Rim was more effective than in North America. For example, dark-skinned Brazilians are either native Brazilians or Africans brought over during the slave trade years. They speak Portuguese, and no one questions their nationality. They are Brazilian. A dark-skinned person from Haiti speaks Creole, and we all know him to be a Haitian even though his family came from Africa many years ago. Jamaica is the same. African people who speak a cool broken English and live on a beautiful Caribbean island are called Jamaican. But their history lies in Africa. Now we move to the North American continent, and it isn't that easy. An African was not allowed to assimilate because of the strength of the myth of white supremacy.

The melting pot concept has not worked well for nonwhite people. The degree to which it has worked is also connected to the actual color and shade of skin and the ethnicity of the individual being denied. For instance, Asians are allowed more melting-pot space than Hispanics, who are given more room than Africans. Is this because the skin of Asians is not quite as dark, or is it because we believe Asians are more advanced, more intelligent than those "dirty Mexicans" who work in the fields or build buildings?

Ethnicity and skin color both operate under the myth of white supremacy. Native North Americans were perhaps denied assimilation to the same degree as Africans because of the threat of their claim to the land. A case could also be made that these original landowners of the Americas wanted no part of assimilation. The white settlers who came to America from Europe eventually stole the land belonging to the Indians. Instead of assimilation, our founding fathers practiced annihilation. This problem is everywhere on the planet and the myth is consistently believed across the world.

A recent response from one of the elders at Christ Community Church to the idea of apology and repentance for our southern Presbyterian church's role in slavery was, "Do you think England owes Scotland an apology for Anglo-Saxon persecution of the Celtic Scots, Irish and Welsh?" My answer was yes. Anywhere that ethnic wars have been waged we can make a call for repentance. It happens in every culture, Hutu and Tutsi, Zulu and Xhosas. In the Sudan, Rwanda and Kosovo. In the Far East, Japanese, Koreans, Chinese, Cambodians, Vietnamese, Laotians all war and fight with each other over ethnic superiority. The German and Japanese alliance in World War II declared their races to be superior. India suffers from four thousand years of racism through the caste system. The Holocaust and genocides of all types and in all places reflect this desire to see a particular pedigree as the best, God's chosen, superior, and therefore to be protected at all cost.

How dare anyone claim one race, people group or color of skin to be above another? God created all of us. How dare any of us claim to know the mind of the omnipotent Creator? God forgive us for believing and practicing this myth, this horrible lie from hell. Should we celebrate our ethnic heritage? By all means! Should that alone drive the way we relate to people? No. Our national heritage is now in Christ, the one who created the human race and its diversity of ethnic cultures, inviting all who believe into his body as a new people, a nation of priests, *all* of us one in him.

11   Societies

BIBLICAL STUDY, THEOLOGICAL FORMATION, WORSHIP AS A
lifestyle and care for the disinherited people of our community
merged as the Lord formed a band of committed workers—workers
boldly entering underserved neighborhoods, building Christian societies to meet people's needs through deeds of service.

Facing our communities' needs in Franklin led to establishing
ministries promoting care for the poor and racial reconciliation. They
encourage reneighboring through creative, connectional work and
empowerment through minority leadership development, giving
hope to socially disadvantaged minorities in our city. Though our
community is not perfect, these organizations give a sense of flesh
and blood, muscle and sinew, to the hope we have in Christ. They are
examples of the kind of real work necessary to move from passive,
individual acceptance of salvation to a true community experience of
Christ's gift.

For our family, the move into Hard Bargain culminated the teaching we were receiving about how the gospel transforms lives. When
we spoke of our hearts being changed to the degree that we would

desire to move from Meadowgreen to Hard Bargain, it could only be through the Holy Spirit's empowerment. God revealed our successes not so much as financial summits, but rather hilltops of the heart. Rich or poor, all of us needed to be loved. It was time our family of faith saw the way provided by Jesus to help empower those without resources, vision, hope and possibilities. Our church as a committed fellowship and community of care, pooled resources, assessed the needs, and established not-for-profit societies designed to meet those needs.

As my musical career diminished in the late 1980s I recorded and released several albums that expressed my understanding of mercy and the call to work among the poor. The first recording, titled *City Limits,* was about the city, featuring the song "Sacrificing Love" with a theme of caring for the poor. *Within My Reach* focused on the ideas taking root in our fellowship that what God was calling us to do was love each one placed in front of us. It addressed questions like who are the least and the lost within arm's reach of our day-to-day lives. The answer reminded us it wouldn't take a lot to move into the neighborhoods if we could see each day as an opportunity to love the uncovered individuals placed divinely in our path.

The third recording, *Brother to Brother,* was an expression of thanks to my brother, Jeff, for all the care and compassion he gave to me in the midst of my neediest times. We had lived from our earliest years together through our parents' divorce, the untimely death of our father, and the varieties of disappointments, failures and betrayals that go along with being brothers. In many ways my continuing desire to serve the needs of the poor was sustained by recognizing in Jeff a demonstration of the gospel through his patience and presence in my life. I learned to give by watching my brother give to me. Michael Card helped me record the album. His ability to listen to my confessions of failures brought the love and forgiveness of Jesus down to earth. The bond we share after years of life together is like an unbreakable marriage brother to brother.

The result of this bonding process led to a fifteen-year movement of building Christian societies designed to bring us together. We were rich and poor, majority and minority, skilled and unskilled, every neighbor needing the other. What follows is a list and description of the various ministries and not-for-profits that emerged through the years of relationship building. The work was plentiful, representing a combination of talent, resources and willingness to care on all sides. It was not some top-down project pulled off because the rich took pity on the poor. If anything was true, it was that there really weren't any "rich" but rather an entire fellowship and community of the poor in spirit. Our poverty and need showed just how much Jesus loved to rescue his people.

To help empower disinherited people, our committed fellowship of care developed relationships, weaving together neighbors from all the communities into specific Christian societies. These ministries and programs demonstrated how Jesus used his people in both word and deed. The economically disadvantaged neighborhoods were entered simply out of the love expressed through Christ to his children. This overflow of grace and mercy was a response to the despair created through social injustice.

A movement is going on in Franklin, a movement into the neighborhoods where the servants are needed. A movement from the brokenness of our constant failure, our Hard Bargains, to the foot of the cross and the only one able to save, heal and restore. The movement he makes toward us is what fuels our movement toward him. Our hearts are extended to those who are different and the truth of redemption is carried by the loving relationships Jesus has formed in us to the streets of the disinherited.

THE STOREHOUSE MINISTRY

Systems To Elevate People, or the STEP program, was conceived by a social justice group in Dallas, Texas, doing community development. We borrowed methods they promoted and called it the Storehouse Ministry. Deacon Steve Lowry and a number of my other deacon brothers at Christ Presbyterian Church initiated and implemented the program, intending to help anyone with a need. In a typical day, the Storehouse Ministry took care to do background searches and information gathering to give to those who truly had valid financial needs. They would advise and walk with those whose lives were struggling as the result of bad choices or were simply looking to our large, wealthy church for a handout.

As we later formed the new church in Franklin, we brought with us this storehouse concept, which still exists as one of the community's most viable ministries. After fifteen years, its various directors and leaders, paid staff and volunteers have enough stories to fill volumes of books about the grace of God overflowing through intentional care for the poor. Many relationships we have today have grown out of this special work of Jesus. I'm certain the racial, economic and denominational reconciliation we enjoy is due in some part to the Storehouse Ministry's successful work.

An African American woman named Terry Norris coordinates the Storehouse Ministry housed in the Franklin Community Center. Her assistant was another African American, Tyheesia Thomas Esmond, who lived in the Carrie Wilson House owned by the Empty Hands Fellowship. Both of these remarkable developers live in Hard Bargain, Tyheesia on Glass Street and Terry on Mt. Hope. One of our former coordinators of the Storehouse Ministry, Valery Caldwell, started as an assistant in the ministry and worked her way into the coordinator's position and then on to a job with the Tennessee Department of Human Services.

For fifteen years the Storehouse Ministry has served the residents of Williamson County, caring for walk-up clients who need rent money, utilities, emergency financial relief, advice about marital problems and a willing ear to listen to their struggles. One of the recent innovations that complies with an understanding of how best to work together is the Storehouse's request of each client, volunteer and staff member. It is the question "What can you give back to Storehouse?" Even the poorest of the poor, the neediest of the needy have gifts, talents and resources that can contribute to empowerment. The Bible's teaching about the widow's mite is a principle translated into "We all have something to offer," "We all give and take together." If this sounds socialistic or communistic, remember this is not a forced benevolence. This is God's people willingly surrendering to the Lord and to each other for the sake of Jesus' kingdom.

Another feature of the Storehouse Ministry is the depth of the volunteer structure, which includes people from the many different churches in our county. Primitive, Missionary and Southern Baptists, African Methodist Episcopal, United Methodists, Presbyterians, Episcopalians, Roman Catholics and inter- or nondenominational churches all contribute to Storehouse's success. The Storehouse Ministry consistently deals with Williamson County's need for higher quality, affordable homes. There is also a lack of transitional safe housing to protect people coming out of abusive situations. The Storehouse runs a transitional home called the Hope House. Families live there after leaving our very capable Franklin Public Housing, operated by Peggy Dugman, Wanda Steele Bond and other social caretakers. After their transition at Hope House, they head into either a Habitat for Humanity house or a dwelling under the care of the Housing Partnership of Williamson County, another not-for-profit that Pam Dugger, Hester Hamilton and their fine staff oversee.

FRANKLIN COMMUNITY MINISTRIES

The Franklin Community Ministries works alongside the Storehouse Ministry and is also housed in the Franklin Community Center. The origin of this umbrella ministry dates back to the early 1990s. Paige Overton was the first director, and through her strong leadership and the answered prayers of early strategic prayer groups many relationship-driven ministries have emerged. Cady Wilson now coordinates FCM. She and her husband, Mike, have been involved with FCM since its beginning. Their family also has modeled international adoption as care for the poor. Mike Wilson's work as a deacon and engineer has advanced the housing rehab effort to a new level of development through the neighborhood renewal ministry. With a master's degree in education, Cady was a driving force and helpful architect of the Eagles tutoring program. Countless workers and volunteers over the years have given to the outreach of FCM, not only through the Storehouse but also through each of its affiliated ministries.

EAGLES

The Eagles tutoring program has been critical in meeting needs of children in the Williamson County public school system and in the Franklin City Special School District. Pairing tutors with students in first through eighth grades lets the children have mentors working with them on schoolwork as well as other areas of life. This effort is essential to community development and gives access to families and relationships unlike any other program. If you truly care for children's needs you will find support from parents translating into an opening for needs to be revealed and met. Parents respond when their children are genuinely being loved.

The current coordinator for the Eagles program, Debbie Barnett, is an expert minister among students. She brought creative ideas to the ministry, including a café-styled hangout on the top floor of the Franklin Community Center. Graduates of the Eagles program over the years have done well in finishing their high school educations, some going on to college. The hard truth, however, is that many of our students do not finish high school. Some unfortunately are incarcerated at the local jail, addicted to alcohol and drugs, or have dropped out of sight.

THE WILLIAMSON COUNTY JAIL MINISTRY

The Williamson County jail ministry began through the work of the Gideons. Their faithful witness to prisoners brought much fruit over the years. Bob Smith's faithful oversight of the work has spanned the past several decades, and his abilities to preach and teach have blessed hundreds of inmates over the years. The more recent connectional team approach, bringing jail ministry into a network that includes Storehouse, Eagles and other development agencies, has helped to meet the needs of prisoners and their families holistically. After hearing about a young inmate's wife who was struggling to keep her kids in school and couldn't pay bills, the FCM coordinator got involved and found a tutor for the children through Eagles and financial support through the Storehouse Ministry.

SAFE HARBOR

A similar work among young single women who were pregnant without support or any substantial help was called Safe Harbor. New Hope Academy third-grade teacher Kathy Peabody and Doreena, Pastor Chris Williamson's wife, pioneered this vital ministry and made great headway in education, care and real love for these teenagers in crisis. The local Crisis Pregnancy Support Centers worked well with Safe Harbor and eventually absorbed the ministry. Even though the public work of Safe Harbor ended, the relationships continued to grow as some of the wonderful children born through the program over the years became students at New Hope Academy and the Eagles program.

GRACE WORKS

Another noteworthy program that involves volunteers from many walks of life in Franklin is Grace Works. It is an ecumenical not-for-profit led by Cheryl King with a great staff working to aid disadvantaged families. They do a clothing closet with affordable retail items and a food pantry where any persons, no matter what their situation, can receive goods from the well-stocked grocery. The purpose of the thrift store is to remain affordable while providing quality and carefully screened merchandise. The thrift store has had a great track record financially, proving that co-ops can be successful and should always be included in community development strategies.

It wasn't long after FCM joined John Perkins's Christian Community Development Association that we were introduced to the ministry of Tom and Barbara Skinner. Tom's amazing legacy of CCD and his architectural prowess through the civil rights battles of the '60s and '70s taught us so much about patience and waiting on the Lord while remaining prepared and ready when shown a direction to go. Barbara has continued to carry out her late husband's great work, preaching racial reconciliation and empowerment of the disinherited. She always brings fresh ideas that help us understand that we are in this ministry until "death do us part." By their own admission even veteran developers like Tom and Barbara Skinner had a long way to go. We took heart knowing there is much to learn and that every day provided an opportunity for us to grow in God's grace and mercy. We must always keep a learner's mentality. We have much more to understand if we are to continue being effective. Anything is possible if we don't care if anyone but God gets the credit. If we are open to learn from anyone we will be able to build relationships of love, and the Lord will use that in our communities.

TAPESTRY

Out of our budding cross-racial calling and continual relationships with people like Barbara Skinner grew a ministry called Tapestry. It was to be for women, and again Paige Overton, along with her dear friend Laverne Holland, were the initiators. They began the work with a small enthusiastic group of ladies desiring to grow together by understanding each other to a deeper degree. Women like my wife Linda, Francis Patton, Karthi Masters, Valery Caldwell and others could not have been more different; however, in Jesus they came together as sisters. They met in each other's homes through the year, ending each term celebrating with a citywide luncheon that drew over three hundred women from all over Williamson County. Barbara Skinner brought a challenging message on racial reconciliation, creative connectional reneighboring, and empowerment of the disinherited. A substantial number of Spanish-

Laverne Holland, Paige Overton Pitts and Francis Patton.

speaking women attended a recent Tapestry luncheon, reflecting the expanding work of the Spirit to include not just white and black people but also Native Americans, Hispanics and Asian Americans.

NEIGHBORHOOD RENEWAL

I mentioned earlier the neighborhood renewal ministry designed to rehab existing homes in the low-income neighborhoods. This ministry does mostly carpentry work, overseen by skilled foremen and performed by volunteers from the community of care. Each time a house was rehabbed, the homeowners became involved in the project in some way. Often they would provide lunch or actually get on the rooftop and ladders, lending a hand.

The relationships developed through the NR ministry have been critical to our ongoing creative relocation. The director of the NR ministry, Peter Volpitta, discovered our home in Hard Bargain for us in 1997. Pastor Pete, now a corporate chaplain in Williamson County, spent several years developing the NR ministry. The NR ministry continues to grow and the leadership has been passed to a variety of foremen who keep it going through rehabilitating homes.

NEW HOPE ACADEMY

The flagship of Christian Community Development (CCD) in Franklin, Tennessee, is the private classical elementary school New Hope Academy (NHA). It is a school designed to bring economically disadvantaged students together with middle- and upper-income students. It also focuses on racial reconciliation, which is evident in its 50/50 ratio of majority culture with minority culture. The school building is located strategically near the under-managed neighborhoods of Franklin, but it also is in an area marked for growth in the city's future.

For several years headmaster Dr. Anthony Gordon, an African

New Hope Academy's students and staff.

American, along with community developer Laverne Holland, his assistant, made up the school's staff. The one-hundred-plus students reflect all walks of life in Franklin and Williamson County. It is the coming together of diverse families, some paying full tuition, some paying very little tuition.

The classical education is achieved through the NHA curriculum as well as in its teaching methodology. For instance, the small number of students in each class, all dressed in New Hope Academy uniforms, 50/50 advantaged with disadvantaged, all under the tutelage of one teacher, has put the school on the map as unique among community educational development concepts. Stuart Tutler is the current headmaster continuing to lead the school toward quality education and racial reconciliation.

This school is strategic in our community because many underserved children are failing in most of the traditional schools. The foundation for verbal skills is not there, and no one seems to have the answer on how to develop it through traditional private or public education. New Hope Academy starts with pre-K four-year-olds, hoping to give single working moms the opportunity to increase the chances for their children's success. The intention is to help these children receive a great education by supporting language skills right from the start.

I have seen the school's vision come to fruit firsthand with my son, Sam. I am expected to be a proud parent, but if you ask Sam about Plato's *Republic* or listen to him pray in Latin, you would agree that New Hope Academy has given him vision for a real future. With this foundation laid in the first six grades of school, the chances for the children to succeed rises greatly. The reasons many people in our underdeveloped neighborhoods drop out of life usually stem from weak educational opportunities. Education in the current dominant culture is everything. It opens doors like nothing else and is the key for any member of our community to succeed in providing housing, food, clothing and other needs for their families.

Paige Overton was the founder and first headmistress of New Hope Academy. Mostly she was the person who had the vision to see classical education wed with strategic care for the poor. She realized that a school for economically disadvantaged families was essential to our growing CCD dream. The genius of her insights came to the surface when she linked historic classical education with under-empowered neighborhood needs. That linking helps develop a new community character by bringing into the school arena representative members of Franklin's cultural and ethnic makeup. Rich and poor, internationals, Native Americans, African Americans, Hispanics, Asians and whites have all been at New Hope Academy. Over the past two-and-a-half years my wife, Linda, has taught first grade at New Hope Academy.

New Hope Academy teacher Linda Roley with some of her first-grade students.

It was clear that if CCD was going to happen it would be through the church. It should be obvious to the reader that the southern evangelical church suffers from racial segregation. It is not popular to say that publicly, because no one wants segregation of the races to prevail in society, especially in the Christian church. Most dominant culture evangelicals know that segregation is sin, but few believe preferential segregation is sin as well. Nevertheless, the Lord's will seems to be bringing his people into union with him, drawing us into relational harmony as we go. The challenge the church must accept is to move forward making the changes. Sooner or later it will be unacceptable for segregated white churches to worship each Sunday next to segregated black churches. I realize this is idealistic and that assimilation and integration of the church is possibly generations away, but there has to be a beginning in each of our communities in order for us to look back and say we battled racism and segregation with all our resources and abilities. Again, it is only by the grace of God that we see the benefits of shared ministry and life.

STRONG TOWER BIBLE CHURCH

The answer to a shared church life in Franklin was to plant an intentionally mixed-race congregation. Christopher Wesley Williamson, or Pastor Chris as he has come to be known, was the visionary pioneer who led the way in planting Strong Tower Bible Church. He started in the early 1990s as an intern with FCM. However, from the beginning it was clear he was called to be a pastor. After much prayer and strategizing, he launched a youth program and Bible study that paved the way for the church. To this day it remains the clearest demonstration of racial reconciliation and is 50/50 in its black/white percentages. He continues to serve with a mixed-race staff, and the congregation is among the most active church bodies in the CCD movement in Franklin. Many of the volunteers in the not-for-profit Christian societies in town come from the Strong Tower Bible Church. Pastor Chris and his wife, Doreena, have been raised up by Jesus to show us how to battle racism and denominational segregation.

EMPTY HANDS FELLOWSHIP

Along with Strong Tower Bible Church and Tapestry is the racial reconciliation ministry known as the Empty Hands Fellowship (EHF). As I've described in earlier chapters, this group of men meets twice weekly to develop relationships across race, denomination and economic differences.

MERCY CHILDREN'S CLINIC

One day a group of Empty Handers gathered in front of a run-down building near FMBC, the "gateway to the ghetto." Pastor Denny Denson led us in prayer petitioning God that he might build a ministry that would bring glory to himself and service to others. We were witnessing a foreclosure auction. Businessmen and realtors stood all around us as the auctioneer barked out the price it would take to buy the run-down former carpet store. Several of these prominent citizens and cultural leaders of Franklin asked us, the EHF, why we were praying and obviously so interested in the property. Our answer was we were hoping for a location to house the recently created but homeless Franklin Classical School. The coalition of buyers, moved by our response, proceeded to acquire the site and then challenged us to come up with a rental contract, fair to everyone, and hopefully helpful to Franklin Classical School's work.

As it turned out, Franklin Classical School made other arrangements with Hewitt Sawyer's congregation at the WHPBC and moved into the church's basement that fall. So providentially, Dr. Timothy Henchel and administrator Norman Haynes secured the former carpet store for the future home of a newly organized walk-up pediatric clinic designed to bring affordable health care to the several thousand uninsured children within walking distance. The Mercy Children's Clinic story is one of miracle after miracle. Just like New Hope Academy, Graceworks, FCM, etc., it was about God using his people to bring vision, resources and community members together to build a lasting and remarkable ministry.

Dr. Tim's vision was to offer neighborhood patients easy access to a facility with kind, courteous, professionals providing great service to those in need. All races are represented among the growing number of doctors and staff members at the Mercy Children's Clinic, and the state-of-the-art doctor's office draws families from a half-dozen counties across middle Tennessee. Development director Brant Bousquet and social worker Sharon McCallum are making wonderful progress in racial reconciliation. Like New Hope Academy, the Mercy Children's Clinic caters to clientele from every financial situation possible. There has been a wonderful international tie between the MCC and the Living Hope Center in Cape Town, South Africa, where HIV/AIDS recovery work is being done, demonstrating connectional faith-based community initiatives.

FRANKLIN HOUSE STUDY CENTER

Michael Card is a treasure. He has brought the integrity of the gospel to millions of people around the world through his songwriting, recordings, live performances, radio shows, books, articles, lectures and weekly Bible studies. As a singer-songwriter he has no competitors. His use of Scripture and the insights he finds there stem from an exceptional mind, an amazing work ethic, a great education, and the providential wonder of a mentor named Bill Lane. Dr. Lane walked with Michael Card for six years of his formal education and another twenty years in personal friendship and discipleship. Bill Lane was a Harvard scholar devoted to biblical studies and the development of Christian men. Some of his boys, as he called them, were scholastic geniuses like himself; others were simply men with hearts yearning to love the Lord and their fellow man. Bill was great with both groups, helping them all to develop both sides, bright hard-working minds with large, wide-open hearts!

With Michael Card's support, Dr. Lane brought his 10,000-plus-volume biblical studies library to Franklin, Tennessee, in the late 1990s. He placed the books on the shelves of a custom-built den in a lovely Main Street cottage known as the Franklin House Study Center. Following Bill's death, Michael and Susan Card maintained the house and study center. They continued Dr. Lane's dream and legacy of rich Bible study by providing a welcoming atmosphere to a dedicated fellowship of men and woman growing in God's grace and mercy.

The Empty Hands Fellowship greatly benefited from the FHSC. Minority pastors and lay leaders whose book budgets were nonexistent found the extensive library irreplaceable, opening up ideas and ways of thinking through resources that were inaccessible in the past. CCD has in its scope a new level of intellectual stimulation through FHSC as well as other educational institutions which are intentionally open to minority leadership striving to care for the poor. Recently, books from the FHSC have been moved to the FMBC.

FRANKLIN CLASSICAL SCHOOL

Dr. George Grant, whose Bannockburn College and Franklin Classical School have contributed to the growth of our community's understanding of global cultures, mission opportunities, Western European humanities, and a score of other subjects, has been a blessing to our city and community life. Specific minority cultural studies are being organized through a Minority Leadership Development program, with the hope of providing scholarships and support to young leaders who desire to work among the poor. Both Dr. Grant's programs and the FHSC, along with some local church resources, are vital to this critical piece of CCD. The establishing of classical Christian schools in northern Iraq by Dr. Grant and Servant Group International is another example of community development extending beyond Franklin. A vital ministry, the Art House, has contributed to the ongoing discovery of how the arts function in community development. Its director, Charlie Peacock, is a well-known artist, author, musician and producer.

James Isaac Elliott, whose wisdom and writing abilities have been invaluable to me, remarked that it's exciting to see how many outstanding writers, teachers, speakers, pastors, educators, scientists, social workers, community developers, managers, artists, theologians, philosophers, and business people are living and serving together in Franklin, Tennessee. They seem to have a similar and central theme, which is seeing themselves as sinners saved by grace. What James saw was a group of people actually giving something back to the community, seeing themselves as poor in spirit alongside those who are in true material poverty. What is remarkable is they are willing to give up their positions of power and the applause of recognition, sharing the credit with one another, and always pointing to God as the one who has done it. James is correct that true revival is in progress and it isn't a religious thing. It is a love for people who are different. It is the result of God's rich love to us, the ones so estranged from God and cut off from a relationship with him and his love, that it took the death of his only Son on the cross to bring us home.

JERICHO COMMUNITY LAW OFFICE

Another way of entering the neighborhoods is through the legal justice system. As Dr. Anthony Gordon pointed out, the oppression of racial preferencing appears clear when comparing courts' actions toward white teenagers versus nonwhite teenagers.

I personally observed an African American young man with no criminal record who lived on my street sentenced to a year in jail without probation because he was sitting in a car where police officers found marijuana. He was charged with possession of an illegal substance. He spent nine months in the Williamson County jail. The very same situation happened to a white friend's son. That young man spent the weekend locked up waiting for his arraignment, though when his time came to be charged, he was released because he was intending to be in college in a few weeks. It seemed to satisfy the judge that this young man was not a threat to society, unlike the other young man who was not headed to school, but rather to a minimum wage job at McDonald's or Wendy's.

All any of us want is that these young people be judged equally without bias, and that clearly did not happen. Cases like that and others are now reviewed by very capable attorneys working pro bono. D. J. Davis, a gifted student recently out of law school, intended to give disinherited people a legal voice and be an aggressive advocate battling for them in the Williamson County legal justice system. She formed the Jericho Community Law Office, which was housed in the FCC. D. J., along with her volunteer staff of advocates for the poor, defended clients in all kinds of situations. A new executive director of the JCLO, Lynn Owens, has joined her. The network of attorneys they developed willing to do work for reduced fees has been a blessing to the neighborhoods of need.

In the fall of 2003 Tom Miller was elected mayor of Franklin. He is a member of Christ Community Church and Empty Hands Fellowship. He was elected by a narrow margin, defeating a fourteen-year incumbent. It was a definite signal that Franklin is changing.

Without justice the poor remain helpless and hopeless. They cry out for us to join in and elect fair judges, aldermen, mayors and county officials who stand for unbiased justice. Recently it was said among the people who live in my neighborhood that "the black man is buried in Mt. Hope cemetery (Toussaint L'Ouverture cemetery to be exact) but he dies in Hard Bargain." The statement was a reference to what the long battle for fairness and justice has led to, revealing a frustrated response to endless years of persecution and oppression.

SHADES TO CLEAR

Many agencies, secular and civic, have helped the cause of empowering the disinherited. These include a network of wonderful Rotary clubs, the Tennessee Department of Human Services, and Franklin's Heritage Foundation, with its vast preservation resources. This network recently cooperated with the Williamson County African American Historical Society's project of remodeling the McLemore House, the home of a local resident converted into a museum in Hard Bargain. The house commemorates the life of the former slave Harvey McLemore and his family's vivid history.

The Williamson County Parks and Recreation Department has done marvelous work with a variety of parks and recreation centers. The Boys' and Girls' Clubs also run a vital program in Franklin. The Franklin YMCA has a staff with a definite heart for the poor, and one of their young African American employees has been especially effective among young minority students in the local high schools. Russell Hardeman has developed a ministry called Shades To Clear (STC), which encourages young gang members from African American and Hispanic backgrounds to meet together, putting aside their differences to talk about what they have in common. The yearly STC retreats have become popular because of intense time together developing real relationships. The retreats present the gospel as the only lasting answer to the hatred between races, and many of these students come to the Lord, finding new friendships with each other. Russell joined the staff of Christ Community Church as the first minority pastoral intern.

BAREFOOT REPUBLIC

Recently Russell linked up with area churches to provide an opportunity for minority students to attend a camp being promoted as a summer experience for young people intentionally across races, denominations and economic status. The camp, known as The Barefoot Republic, is another example of creative empowerment. Students re-

ceive opportunities to see and do things that until now lay outside
their reach of experience. Tommy Rhodes and his staff have worked
diligently for the kids. Could it be these marvelous teenagers, who
intuitively know that all of us are "barefooted" orphans in need of
some humility, are challenging the proud and the faithless to give up,
give in and give back? Our neighborhoods are filled with young people who desire to change the way things have always been and to
usher in a new Franklin, a new South, and a new people full of the
love of God.

COMMUNITY DEVELOPMENT NETWORK

One of the special developers in Franklin over the past five years is
Beth Barnard Barcus. She grew up as a mercy minister in the community church and, as a young volunteer with FCM, served in nearly every ministry, modeling leadership to all. As its director she helped
bring the Storehouse work to its full potential and was the key visionary in the founding of the Community Development Network. This
co-op of urban ministries working alongside secular programs has
grown into a one hundred-plus-member organization. Each year
there has been a special CDN luncheon where ministries and organizations communicated with one another, explaining what they did
and how they helped meet the needs of the underserved in Williamson County and Franklin, Tennessee.

ERACE: ELIMINATING RACISM AND
CREATING EQUALITY

The ERACE Foundation, run by director John Maguire, has influenced
Franklin through its promotion and sponsorship of events working to
end the racialized society of Williamson County. The biyearly go-cart
race through the streets of Franklin raises awareness and money for

important organizations battling racism. John Maguire and the ERACE Foundation have become important to the EHF as the propaganda wing of the brotherhood. We would have a less effective presence across the community if the professional work of the ERACE foundation were not behind our movement.

FRANKLIN COMMUNITY CENTER

One final ministry, which in some ways ties many of these together, is actually a physical structure, a building. It is the Franklin Community Center, which sits at the corner of Third Avenue South and Church Street in Franklin. It is a wonderful facility with a nineteenth-century chapel and a three-level building from the 1930s attached with office suites and room for several important Christian societies. Cady Wilson and the FCM staff have headquarters there, along with Tapestry, Eagles and the Storehouse Ministries.

The chapel also houses the Harp of Zion Church, the oldest Spanish-speaking church in Williamson County. This expression of Jesus' body is pastored by Jerry Ruiz. The historic chapel serves the community as an ideal place for small weddings, worship celebrations, conferences, concerts and gatherings. The community center is also home to Jericho Community Law Office and African Leadership, led by career missionary Larry Warren, who directs and oversees a seminary program with over four thousand African national pastors in twenty-plus African countries.

Housed within the AL office is the Williamson County Refugee Resettlement ministry of William Mwizerwa, an African refugee himself who heads up the work of resettling hundreds of displaced people from Africa, Asia and the Middle East in middle Tennessee. Also in the FCC is the office of Ermon Lature, who runs the Williamson County Habitat for Humanity. This nationally known work is vibrant in our area, building more than ten homes a year, on average, in Franklin and Williamson County. The need for affordable housing is at a point of crisis, as we see less and less new housing devoted to the economically disadvantaged. Habitat for Humanity is one answer to the crisis, and we thank God for their strong presence in our community.

The empowerment of the disinherited leads God's people into neighborhoods full of potential. Maybe what we learned through all of this was what Christian martyr Dietrich Bonhoeffer meant when he said "Jesus bids us come and die."[1] Were we finally listening to the Lord who said "deny yourself take up the cross and follow me"? Looking back on the story of what God has done in Franklin, not one thing seems possible through any human effort.

Adoptions, Christian societies, growing relationships—all mean nothing if they are simply some grand attempt to make someone out there finally love us. What is meaningful is the way the gospel drives us in faith to our Savior. All this activity was designed to push us to Jesus. We are the beggars, and he is the Bread of Life. We are the ones dying of thirst, and he is the Living Water. We need the community more than the community needs us.

Luke 6:27-36 is Jesus' command for us to love not only those who are different from us but also those who are our enemies. In some ways the rich and the poor are natural enemies. People of varying races or ethnicity war because of their differences. Instead of celebrating our diversity we fight each other, widening the gulf between us. The hope of reconciliation and bridging the gap between rich and poor shines brightly as we place our faith in Christ. He loved us who were his enemies and reconciled us to himself.

In Jesus, diverse people find common themes uniting them. First, we are made in God's image as his creation, bearing that image each and every day. Second, we sense his goodness in creation and have imaginations that instinctively remind us of God's care, love and perfection. Third, we recognize in Christ that the Fall of Adam and Eve was a real event resulting in suffering consequences of sins, especially through the unhealthy divisions of people groups. The brokenness of our hearts individually is compounded through sins committed as nations, ethnic groups and societies. We know right from wrong, and when we are honest we acknowledge a longing to see failing relationships rescued. We want a liberator, someone to free us from the pain and hopelessness. We are longing for abundant life and especially an afterlife full of security and peace. Realizing our ultimate unity and bringing the hope of reconciliation to light requires not only prayer and love but concrete, intentional physical action to meet the needs of those around us.

Jesus, the harvester of souls, has come for us. He has entered the neighborhoods of need in this vast world and found us. He shows us that we are ripe with sin, not righteousness. We are full of self-protecting defenses, not great charitable hearts. Could it be that realizing our hopeless condition is what opens the door to true relationships, placing us fully shoulder to shoulder with the least and the lost? Tomorrow the sun will rise, and there will be more children left orphaned, more rehab needed, more houses built and more students taught. What there won't be is a lack of the love needed to answer these heartaches. The love of God in Christ never ends.

Conclusion

THE LINCOLN MEMORIAL LOOKED MYSTICAL IN THE EVENING light—like a place where miracles happen. Not a lot had changed in twenty-nine years, according to my short-circuiting memory. I was standing on or near the spot where, along with my Dad and brother Jeff, I had watched Martin Luther King Jr. deliver his famous speech so long ago. Back then I was an anxious observer wondering what might happen next. Now it was Abraham Lincoln who seemed to be watching me as he peered through the shafts of light between the massive front pillars.

The building made me feel generous and forgiving, as if it had been erected to celebrate my ability to hold a country together in the midst of great misunderstanding and hatred, the way President Lincoln and Dr. King had. I was the one at the top of those steep stairs with the best seat in the house looking out over our beloved Capitol, my boyhood home. It was as if I could see the reflection of Washington's monument on the pool between the two memorials pointing to some kind of realization not only about my hopes for success, but also my understood failures. I was that person creating misunderstanding. I was full of hatred toward certain people, with a poison flowing out of the darkness of my heart. There seemed to be a pre-destined circle I had traveled that was tight enough for me to walk alone and loose enough to include my precious friends. There are so many fellow travelers whom I couldn't see when I started out but whose presence was now escorting me to my journey's end.

With me in Washington that spring evening was my youngest son Sam, a handsome, sturdy thirteen-year-old sixth grader. He is the last of our five children and the baby of the family. His strong athleticism allows him to play well at all sports, but football and basketball especially bring out his tenacity and skill. He is a bright student, a fine artist and gifted writer. A lot of his educational foundation came through New Hope Academy. He attended first through sixth grade there and emerged from our wonderful school with vision and the ability to learn. Not every school can claim that kind of success.

This night we were in D.C. touring our nation's capital as part of the New Hope Academy annual sixth-grade trip. Standing alongside us was Dr. Anthony Gordon. As headmaster of NHA he had agreed to chaperone the trip. As my close friend and an African American, Dr. Gordon held lively ongoing discussions with me concerning race, reconciliation and the gospel and how those issues touched every area of life. My son loved Dr. Gordon because he took time to ask Sam questions, wait for the answers and speak wisdom into his life. Anthony Gordon knew how to motivate young black men.

Dr. Gordon was keenly interested in the King speech from 1963, and so with Sam standing next to me just like I had been with my father so long ago, I described the scene. Pointing across the road to the place where King stood, I waved my arms wildly, hoping to recapture the passion of the moment that hot August day. Observers might have thought I was an orchestra leader in the midst of some fast-paced concert. Little did they know that the directing I was doing related to invisible people from another time period packed together like the lines at Disney World, standing in normally off-limits areas of plush grass or street pavement. During King's speech I remember looking down from my perch and thinking, no one ever stands in the middle of the street, only buses, cabs and cars drive over this blacktop, and the pedestrian crosswalk was way over there. I wondered if Dad or my brother Jeff realized no one in their right mind ever stood there.

That was a moment preserved in time, packed with hope for change. This warm spring night in Washington with my son and his mentor gave the impression that once again we were on unfamiliar ground with the statue of President Lincoln coming alive to say our world still needed changing.

The monuments seemed animated as Sam, Anthony Gordon and I wondered what a resurrected Dr. King would say to us. What would be different if he gave another speech? In some ways we thought it would be exactly the same. His dream would still need to be dreamed, still need to be realized. Maybe that's why the memorial was taking on an organic quality. Could the dream be truly coming to life? Could Lincoln and King's legacy be seen as alive in us? Would we be the living monuments to their calling and memory? How could three little men be important in the shadow of those two great men?

Living buildings was not an entirely new idea. Wasn't God calling us his bride, his body, his building? How would the lessons being taught to us as two black men and one white man bind our hearts and commit us forever to dream dreams of equality, ultimately dismantling racial discrimination? We just breathed in the free D.C. air, held hands to pray, and with King's hope in our hearts pledged to do so.

I had a similar experience with my second son Jeff. We had never been to D.C. together, but we did listen to the famous King speech sitting on a bench surrounded by memorabilia from the early '60s at the impressive Civil Rights Institute in Birmingham, Alabama. The Institute was built, according to the brochure, as a "living institution dedicated to viewing the lessons of the past in a positive way to chart new directions for the future."

I had been to the Institute one other time in the mid-1990s as part of a one-day field trip during the Christian Community Development Association's National Conference. Now, several years later, my son Jeff and I were back in Birmingham for the PCA's General Assembly, where an important overture was to be debated.

Some irony emerged from my son's minority status. Jeff is a good-looking, triracial young man from African, Hispanic and Anglo descent with a wonderful head of hair full of tight curls. When we walk together in public, he is always complimented for his unusually wild looks. I call him Sage, a nickname he acquired for demonstrated maturity beyond his fifteen years. Because of our racial history, Jeff and I would probably not have been father and son or Presbyterian brothers a hundred years ago. Society would not have looked favorably on our relationship. He was named for my older brother, Jeffrey Harrison Rea Mac Roley, who was with me and our dad the day King spoke in Washington. This day it was young Jeff, my son, next to me at the Institute with a recording of the speech blaring out those famous words from hidden speakers behind a life-size portrait of Dr. King. Inside my brain was the proud, mystical voice of my Dad saying, "Well done, my son."

The movie-like set was creatively assembled with all the right images preserved and effectively used to try to give the listener the experience of actually being on the Lincoln Memorial steps that day in 1963. We listened in silence, the only patrons in the room at the time. We finished the tour in silence, trying to soak up what we had just witnessed, searching for a category to describe the insights. A new-found freedom swirled around our hearts. It lifted us because we realized the horrors of racism could become part of a past never to be visited again or a present that stayed a way of life. We could choose either path.

King's dream was a reality in our family. Jeff and Sam were united by their African ethnicity. They were also united by the one who is a greater Martin Luther King Jr., a greater Abraham Lincoln and especially a greater earthly Father. His name is Jesus. My brother Jeff and I had the joy of living our lives united as brothers in the Roley family, but more importantly as brothers united in Christ.

This living relationship with Jesus is also fundamental to my sons. They are the living monuments to Lincoln's hope for unity and King's dream of justice. My boys are the living reality of ethnically diverse children loving, learning and playing together. They bring the future hope for a society built by better minds where racial hatred is unheard of and the prayer of Jesus that God's will would be done "on earth as it is in heaven" is a reality. It would be a world that celebrates diversity, one where Thomas Jefferson's words from the U.S. Constitution "all men are created equal" had no unseen asterisk next to them explaining equality as a benefit for the dominant culture only. In the midst of my reflections, I could join the living monuments of Lincoln, Jefferson and King. I could stand with my dad and brother, be present with my sons, family, Dr. Gordon and the committed community—trusting Christ for our futures filled with the wonder and adventure that comes when, by simply waking up, we find the dream to be a reality.

The socially disadvantaged, economically deprived, underserved, undermanaged, disinherited, disenfranchised and underprivileged people of our city used to be called the poor. In Franklin, they live in houses, trailers, apartments and dwellings collected together as neighborhoods with distinctively unusual names. In the early to mid-twentieth century, urban locations like "Beasley Town," "Bucket of Blood," and "Polk Town" swelled with families trying to make ends meet. These and other neighborhoods have since disappeared, as progress claimed their property and new developments in the city unfolded.

However, today in Franklin there still exists the network of related families and neighborhoods that are vital to the health of our city. The "Natchez" community stretches through downtown Franklin with pockets of public housing mixing with traditional neighborhoods to form what residents refer to as "Baptist Neck." First Missionary Baptist Church anchors the front of the community with Limestone Baptist Church holding down the opposite end a mile away. "Hard Bargain," across from vanished "Polk Town," is the oldest African American-owned community in Williamson County. It originally was a subdivision with large lots sold mostly to working-class people who were the backbone of industry in the early days of the city. Since that time, Hard Bargain has been in decline and now has a great need for careful redevelopment to protect its rich and wonderful heritage.

Across the Harpeth River in the northeast section of Franklin is the "Liberty Pike" area with the "Cadet Lane" neighborhood. The Harpeth Hills apartment complex has served the needs of families in transition for many years and recently has become home to an influx of Hispanic neighbors arriving in Franklin regularly and in need of affordable housing. Other Spanish-speaking neighborhoods, trailer parks and apartment complexes have emerged within Williamson County, and serious-minded developers know the future will be found among these Latino friends. Pastor José Duran's church, My Father's House, ministers to the many Spanish-speaking people of Williamson County.

Rolling Meadows has been a stable community on Franklin's south side for years. Much of the city's needed affordable housing lies in this attractive subdivision. Franklin's public housing authority has addressed the need for emergency and transitional housing by making some four hundred units available, renting to families based on their annual income. These units, scattered through the city, are best known by their street names such as Spring Street, Cherokee, Short Court, Reddick and Strahl Streets. Habitat for Humanity has been wise in developing local cul-de-sac communities with a variety of affordable homes. Two such locations are Harris Patton Court and Partnership Circle.

LINDA'S REFLECTIONS

Our move into Hard Bargain was a family move, and my wife Linda's understanding through the process greatly encouraged me. Although it has taken over five years to finish renovations on the house, and she only recently planted her beloved garden, her positive attitude and unending patience continue to amaze me. Linda has never complained about inconveniences, even as she watched many of her friends build or move into their dream homes. She never once despised our calling or envied their success. Here are some of her thoughts about Hard Bargain, which she expressed when I questioned her specifically for this conclusion:

Question: Linda, describe the emotional journey you went through relocating from our home in Meadowgreen to Hard Bargain.

Linda: Mostly there was a fear of the unknown and of what I thought I knew. Those misunderstandings were being replaced with a balance I'd never known before in my life. There has been a deeper understanding of the African American culture, which was only viewed from afar with many misconceptions before the move. After arriving in Hard Bargain, I began to embrace the actual people, which balanced my understanding and helped me steady my emotionally uneven perceptions.

Question: What is life like for you now in Hard Bargain?

Linda: I feel more like a part of a neighborhood, more than in Meadowgreen. I sometimes am unsure what I am to do. Trust takes a long time to establish. I definitely feel like there are people on my street and in my neighborhood that still don't trust me and maybe never will. My desire is to establish more relationships where a foundation of trust can be built through vulnerability and intimate sharing.

Question: Describe what the future of our family looks like in Hard Bargain and what your personal dreams are.

Linda: The future looks like we are staying put and hopefully becoming an integral part of the neighborhood where people can find help and be encouraged. My personal dream is to get to know more of the women of Hard Bargain through times together in our home. I dream of being someone the neighborhood women look forward to seeing. I'm not sure they look at me that way right now.

I think Linda's brief comments reveal much of the truth behind why relocation and reneighboring is so difficult and why so many could never actually see themselves doing it. Trust issues linger over Hard Bargain like the lazy chimney smoke floating above its rooftops. White people who drive down our street and through our neighborhood are selling bad life insurance policies, buying illegal drugs, or giving out needed food to the elderly residents. Nobody stays around long enough to really build trust. Even the "do-gooders" whose intentions are pure are seen through the skeptical eyes of those who wonder why these bearers of mercy with good gifts don't come back more often.

Ignoring the neighborhood is perhaps the worst kind of insult. To judge with your absence the shattered surroundings is like saying no good thing can dwell there. It is a slap to the face of the residents, who are demonstrating faith in ways most affluent places can't. Affluence can breed a self-sufficiency that cancels the need for a savior. If you aren't in trouble; you don't need help. Sticking around means being with people long enough to listen to more than what you expect to hear. It is the satisfying feeling that comes when you ask your neighbor, "Is there more you'd like to say?" and the person's reply is "No, I'm all done." Building trust means the people on the other end of the conversation don't have an agenda or some project in the works, making you the object. Trust comes from time spent, conflicts resolved, intimate sharing, and a host of other loving human activities. It's what Jesus built when he came and dwelt among us.

THE MAN WITH NO NAME

He blended in and looked like fifteen other men who lurked at the end of Glass Street on any given weekend night. He was taller than me, smelling of alcohol and smiling like he had found some new and mysterious treasure. It was midnight on a Friday in April. I slowed down to turn from Ninth Avenue onto Glass Street and heard a yell. I stopped as his shadow, cast by the street light, rose up along the passenger side of my borrowed Davidson County pickup truck. I reached over and popped open the door. He slid in and we exchanged greetings, which ended when he asked if I needed anything. After some give and take of words which clarified his meaning of "anything," I explained that I was just fine, realizing from his perspective a white man driving a vehicle with an out-of-county plate would only be at that corner if indeed he *needed something*.

I wish now that I would have actually tried to buy what he was selling. It seems important to know what the price of dope is on your street. But I didn't lead him on; in fact I was brutally candid. I told him I wasn't there to buy drugs, I was on my way home, and that I was a minister. "I'm the white guy living at the end of the block." Misunderstandings and misdiagnoses plague our underserved communities. After we moved into Hard Bargain curious neighbors would stop to look at our house. As Linda and I conducted the tours we would ask them what they thought of our move. We most often heard the response, "We thought you were an undercover police officer." My answer was to encourage our visitors to tell the neighborhood, "It's much worse. I'm a pastor."

He just hung his head as if his chest were a balloon that had been suddenly popped. I might as well have said, I'm an undercover detective, and you are going to jail. Instead, I told him I was there to be his friend and that I wouldn't turn him in. He was silent. I told him I was infuriated that he chose my street to sell drugs on. I was unhappy that my block was notorious for its drug sales. However, I communicated that I cared about him and would be praying for him. I asked him specifically if there was anything I could do for him that night, and his response was he needed five dollars for beer. The irony of a smiling confident drug dealer whose night's work was so pathetic he needed beer money from the local chaplain knocked me over. I was tempted to say something religious like, if you knew my God and what he offers, you would be chin high in beer money, real self-satisfying work and anything else you seem to lack. Instead I told him I couldn't give him beer money, but that I was available night or day if he needed prayer or help with further attempts to stay sober. I'm sure he later regretted the exchange, especially each time I rolled through the intersection at Ninth and Glass Streets on my way out of Hard Bargain, smiling and waving at him, hoping the gesture was an invitation, but sensing in his eyes a complete indictment. When it was clear our business was done, he quietly slid out the door into the night. It was then that I mentioned my name was Scott. I asked him his name and he said clearly, "I don't have a name." I responded sadly and sincerely, "Yeah, none of us have names at times like this."

What stirred me about the nameless man, the neighborhood drug dealers, the undermanaged, underloved and underrelated, was they represented lifeless people pointing out my failure to love. Could it be I was given chances like Linda humbly asked for, to win the trust of people who didn't like me or want to know me, had no names, no sense of direction or purpose, and no desire to follow the God I loved? It was only by faith and through relationships that these opportunities came to pass.

FAITH-BASED COMMUNITY INITIATIVES

From a man with no name to the most famous name in the world is a startling transition. My time spent with the pusher seemed an unlikely overture to what was about to happen.

In February of 2003 I found myself at a meeting in Nashville to discuss faith-based initiatives with the President, the leader of the free world, and fourteen others. It is his habit to do these roundtables in every city where he speaks. The reason for his visit to Nashville was to address the annual convention of The National Religious Broadcasters. The NRB have traditionally been the communications wing for the conservative right, and every Republican president over the past twenty years has delivered a speech to them. Soon he would be methodically moving from person to person like it was a family reunion and he was there to catch up on each member's business. It must be a quality people in politics are born with or else cultivate like a plush lawn: the sense of knowing who somebody is by looking them in the eyes. Maybe the biblical idea of our eyes being the windows of our souls is a truth that too few of us take advantage of, admiring one another by simply gazing into the eyes. It was as if this friendly President would know our souls were eager to be seen.

Secret Service agents formed a wall of protection, which promoted security in the event terrorists burst into the room and a sense of awe at the power and protection that surrounded our nation's commander in chief. White House liaison officials buzzed around whispering orders, gently directing participants and observers into the various chairs of the prearranged seating, giving everyone a sense of anticipation. President Bush brought with him an entourage of leaders who were the architects of the initiatives designed to bring government dollars into the hands of partnerships and programs that are successful in accomplishing community development.

To be seated close enough to touch the President of the United States immediately brought back my childhood experience at the Kennedy White House. The two events were separated by forty years, accentuating a lifetime of opinion changes which when examined led me to believe both confident presidents had more in common than not. They represented two different political parties, yet both men talked about similar agendas, especially care for the disadvantaged. They were both locked in controversial foreign policy battles, each standing up boldly to their global and ideological enemies. Both of them had won their election to office by the narrowest of margins. It seemed to me that these two could be bookends holding together the volumes of politically moderate bipartisan successes over the past half-century. As political rivals and opponents they actually looked and sounded very much alike. Both had wide open eyes and similar inviting personalities. They made you feel like you were the point.

My introduction to social work in the 1960s was now coming to maturity four decades later. Almost unannounced and without fanfare, he moved quickly and quietly into the room. Before I could really gather it all in, there was President Bush shaking my hand and saying my name as if we were the best of friends. As he spoke I couldn't stop thinking of the allegiance I had pledged to past President John F. Kennedy's agenda, standing for civil rights and the intentional sacrifices to be made by us to bring equality to every disadvantaged fellow citizen. I could swear I was hearing from this current president the same selfless call to ask what I could do for my country and community rather than what it could do for me.

The roundtable discussion began with President Bush explaining his personal journey from alcohol abuser to being alcohol-free. He asked each of us to explain our work and make suggestions to him about how his potential faith-based initiatives could enhance our efforts. He had invited Denny Denson and Paige Overton Pitts (now married to Dan Pitts, son of U.S. Congressman Joseph Pitts) to the discussion as well and would later use our thoughts and words in his speech to the NRB. At the conclusion of the roundtable we moved toward him, keeping him later than scheduled, as the three of us lingered, exchanging personal feelings and insights, enjoying his responses and ideas.

President Bush mentioned his brother, who like me lived in Alexandria, Virginia, near my front-porch-monument-viewing childhood home. He was also curious to find out about Denny's former participation in the Black Panther Party, empathizing that we all have periods of our lives that we'd rather not discuss. He thanked us and headed to the podium on the Opryland Hotel stage where he delivered his speech containing several paragraphs of thoughts from our small band of developers. He called the NRB and a listening national audience to come together and work to empower the economically disadvantaged. The words of the president that day resonated in my heart.

> It's been said that 11:00 a.m. on Sunday is the most segregated hour in America. We all have a responsibility to break down the barriers that divide us. In Scripture, God commands us to reach out to those who are different, to reconcile with each other, to lay down our lives in service to others. And he promises that the fruits of faith and fellowship, service and reconciliation will far surpass the struggles we go through to achieve them. . . .
>
> Right here on the outskirts of Nashville, Tennessee, in Franklin, Tennessee, a conversation between an associate pastor of Christ Community Church [Scott Roley] and the pastor of First Missionary Baptist Church [Denny Denson] began a fellowship that now includes nearly sixty pastors and church members of all different races and denominations [Empty Hands Fellowship]. I know that to be a fact, because I heard them both talk today. Their churches work together to support a medical clinic for poor children [Mercy Children's Clinic].
>
> A legal office [Jericho Law Office] gives free advice; New Hope Academy, a faith-based school where children from different backgrounds study together, learn the classics together. The inspiration for the church [school] told me that her hope was to provide a vision for the children—a vision that was positive and optimistic and clear. She [Paige Overton Pitts] said, it's one thing to teach a child to read, but she wants the literate child to see a better day.
>
> At first, Pastor Denny Denson of the First Missionary Baptist Church—Denny is with us, by the way—was a little wary about

how these very different churches would work together. And here's what he says. He says: there's some walls still there—but they're down low enough that we can just step over them. And then he said this, he said: we are committed to each other to the end. And the Nashville area is better because of it.[1]

Paige Overton Pitts's understanding of the need for vision among those whose only future looked like flipping hamburgers at a local McDonald's, and Denny Denson's statement that in light of Christ's love, the walls of racism that separate us still exist but are low enough now to step over, rang out from the lips of President Bush. We were filled with pride.

And so it was that the U.S. President, before thousands of Americans, heralded this message: the realities of our churches working together and forming relationships is an answer to the need for racial reconciliation, creative connectional reneighboring, and the empowerment of the socially and economically underserved and disadvantaged.

A small school, an insignificant pediatric clinic, a law office designed to be a voice for the least of these, and a band of empty-handed pastors representing the committed community of care were singled out as examples of successful faith-based initiatives by the most powerful citizen in the world. What mattered more would be the words of encouragement used by the Creator of the world reminding us of our citizenship in heaven. How would God describe what we had come to view as *normal* Christianity? Would Jesus say "Well done" or "Depart from me, you never knew me"? Our work was the result of the mercy and grace found in the gospel. We were not trying to accomplish goals designed to make God love us; we were compelled to follow him in word and deed precisely because *he did love us*.

Bush delivered his speech at the NRB in Nashville on February 10,

2003, and he gave the go-ahead for the war in Iraq thirty days later, on March 20. The weight of the decision to engage our troops was obviously upon him during our time with him in Nashville. What seemed remarkable to me was that he had his mind on the needs of the Iraqi people as well as those who live daily under the oppression of racism and cultural elitism right here in America. The agenda was freedom for all cultures. He would in many ways reinforce the idea that because of our national creed and statements of purpose, including trust in God, the U.S. government might be seen as a two-hundred-year-old faith-based experiment still being worked out. In that light, George W. Bush was the leader of a faith-based community initiative that was our system of government with its purpose and doctrine flowing from the U.S. Constitution.

Evil men roam the world, and social justice demands they be arrested. Part of the goal for the war in Iraq served that purpose. The

Scott Roley and Denny Denson at the White House Executive Office Building, Washington, D.C., for a briefing with President Bush on HIV/AIDS issues, July 2003.

justice in Christian community development comes about one person, one family, one house, one street and one neighborhood at a time. Like the Marines securing the city of Baghdad, in the development world a swarm of committed neighbors go door to door in search of the connections and relationships leading to community.

Recently in Hard Bargain the police were cruising through quietly looking for two men who had pulled a bank robbery earlier that day in Nashville. It was interesting to observe the neighborhood reaction, as indeed someone did harbor the fugitives. There was a door-to-door search as police scoured the area. The way I heard about the story was from a newscast showing the economically disadvantaged neighborhood of Franklin where the suspected thieves were thought to be hiding. As I looked closer at the television I recognized *my street* and *my house*. The picture was of a police car moving slowly in front of my home on Glass Street. I jumped up from my dinner at a local restaurant, excused myself and got to Hard Bargain quickly. As it turned out the men made their escape and were apprehended later in another county.

I suppose I tell that story because, though much of life in Hard Bargain is quiet and peaceful, just below the surface a kind of desperation lives. It is like a huge reality balloon easily punctured, blowing up the fragile daily peace. It takes only a small incident to spark furious activity. Drug dealers, thieves, drunks, drug users and just plain knuckleheads show up on occasion and cause trouble. We are striving to see the community cleaned up, and real progress is being made. Ninth Street and Green Street have been repaved recently, and as they laid the asphalt they added street gutters. With the upgrade and renewal of Eleventh Avenue the whole area is becoming more appealing, and there is enthusiasm behind a new Redevelopment Association, which is considering several projects on Mt. Hope Street.

Marvin Lewis Wall lived on Ninth Avenue in Hard Bargain. He passed away recently of a massive heart attack at forty-two years young. It felt tragic. Marvin was a friendly ambassador of Hard Bargain, always willing to stop and talk, which interrupted his fast-paced walking to nowhere. His mother, Annie Ruth, asked me to say a few words of comfort at the funeral. Franklin's Lynn Creek Tabernacle was filled with his friends and family. I was overwhelmed by both sadness and joy, knowing I would not see Marvin again moving up-and-down the less-than-perfect pathways of our community, but realizing he was now walking streets of gold. Another brother gone from Hard Bargain to Mount Hope.

The journey of our hearts into racial reconciliation and community renewal from Hard Bargain to Mount Hope is a moment-to-moment decision to place faith and trust in Christ. It is why we strive for the renewal of our streets, rehabilitation for our crumbling homes and lives, the revival of real relationships among the least and the lost, and redemption for all through our Savior Jesus.

And so, Hard Bargain teaches me to be honest and humble with my desires to be useful and important. It knocks me down for a time until I am raised again. The living examples are my wife, Linda, my children and all those among us who desire a new Franklin and a new South, realizing the dream is impossible without the miracle of a new vision unhindered by racism and economic snobbery. This new view of the world changes the distant vista from the porch of my boyhood home where I could see the Capitol dome, that image representing our freedom and justice, which somehow I knew deep inside was still lacking. The new reality would illuminate an image standing even taller beyond that adolescent sight, the massive sign declaring God's neighborhood—the cross of Christ.

Notes

Introduction
[1]John Perkins, *Let Justice Roll Down* (Ventura, Calif.: Regal, 1976); John Perkins, *With Justice for All* (Ventura, Calif.: Regal, 1982).
[2]Robert D. Lupton, *Return Flight* (Atlanta: FCS Urban Ministries, 1993, 1997).

Chapter 1: King and Kennedy
[1]Martin Luther King Jr. "I Have A Dream" speech, Washington, D.C., August 28, 1963.
[2]In her book *The Kennedy White House Parties* (New York: Viking, 1967) Ann H. Lincoln quotes the First Lady on how much President Kennedy enjoyed the event: " 'I don't know when I have seen the President enjoy himself more,' wrote Mrs. Kennedy to Major W. M. Wingate-Gray. 'The ceremony was one of the most stirring we have ever had at the White House.' "
[3]Dr. Peter A. Lillback, *Freedom's Holy Light* (Bryn Mawr, Penn.: The Providence Forum, 2000).

Chapter 4: Tennessee
[1]The term *racialization* is defined in chapter nine.

Chapter 5: Adoption
[1]The Chapmans named the foundation after their first adopted daughter, Shaohannah who joined their family in 2000. Steven and Mary Beth welcomed Stevey Joy into the family in 2003 and were moved to help others experience the joy of adoption. "Recognizing that adoption is a perfect picture of what God has done for each of us in making us his children through Christ, Shaohannah's Hope has been established to care for orphans by engaging the church and helping Christian families reduce the financial barriers to adoption. . . . It has been our experience that the scriptural mandate of caring for orphans, such as the one found in James 1:27, is really a wonderful invitation to experience God in a profound way by being a part of his sovereign plan for his precious children." Shaohannah's Hope has provided finan-

cial adoption grants to nearly one hundred families. For more information on the foundation you can visit their website: <www.shaohannahshope.org>.

Chapter 7: Empty Hands Fellowship
[1]Flannery O'Connor, Peter S. Hawkins, *The Language of Grace* (New York: Cowley Publications, 1983), p. 25.

Chapter 9: God's Neighborhood
[1]Michael O. Emerson and Christian Smith, *Divided by Faith: Evangelical Religion and the Problems of Race in America* (New York: Oxford University Press, 2000).
[2]John Stott, *Decisive Issues Facing Christians Today* (Grand Rapids, Mich.: Revell, 1990).

Chapter 10: Repentance
[1]Raymond J. Bakke is executive director of International Urban Associates in Chicago, Illinois. He is the author of *The Urban Christian* and *A Theology as Big as the City.*

Chapter 11: Societies
[1]Dietrich Bonhoeffer, *The Cost of Discipleship* (New York: Macmillan, 1963), p. 99.

Conclusion
[1]Remarks of the President at the 2003 National Religious Broadcasters Convention, "President Bush Discusses Faith-Based Initiative in Tennessee," <www.whitehouse.gov/news/releases/2003/02/20030210-l.html>.

Roley family photo at Matt and Kelly's wedding, October 2003. Back row (left to right): Michelle, Brad and Emily. Center: Scott, Kelly and Matt, Linda. Front: Sam, Jeff.

Scott Roley is pastor for missions and outreach at Christ Community Church in Franklin, Tennessee. He also oversees the many activities of Franklin Community Ministries. From 1973 to 1989, he attended Covenant Theological Seminary's extension program in Nashville, Tennessee, and worked as a singer/songwriter, releasing eight albums. He was a contributor to *Morning Light* (Harvest House, 1998). He and his wife, Linda, have five children.

James Isaac Elliott is an assistant professor in the College of Entertainment and Music Business at Belmont University in Nashville, Tennessee. He was a contributing writer for *Definitive Country: The Ultimate Encyclopedia of Country Music and Its Performers* (Perigree/Berkley Publishing Group). Also a songwriter with more than eighty recorded songs to his credit, he has won awards from *American Songwriter Magazine,* the American Society of Composers, Authors and Publishers, and the Gospel Music Association.

Franklin Community Ministries is the local outreach of Christ Community Church into the underserved neighborhoods of Franklin, Tennessee. For more information contact

Scott Roley, Pastor for Missions and Outreach, Christ Community Church,
1215 Hillsboro Road, Franklin, Tennessee 37069.
615.468.2260
scott.roley@christcommunity.org
www.christcommunity.org